The Critical Historian

THE CRITICAL HISTORIAN

by

G. Kitson Clark

Fellow of Trinity College and Reader in
Constitutional History in the University of Cambridge

HEINEMANN
LONDON

1967.

Heinemann Educational Books Ltd
LONDON EDINBURGH MELBOURNE TORONTO
AUCKLAND IBADAN NAIROBI
SINGAPORE JOHANNESBURG
HONG KONG NEW DELHI

ISBN 0 435 32190 0

© G. Kitson Clark 1967
First published 1967
Reprinted 1970

Published by
Heinemann Educational Books Ltd
48 Charles Street, London W1X 8AH
Printed in Great Britain by
Morrison and Gibb Ltd
London and Edinburgh

To all those who, whether in school or college, have
the great responsibility of teaching history

Contents

Et veritas manet et invalescit in aeternum, et vivit et obtinet in saecula seculorum. Nec est apud eam accipere personas, neque differentias; sed quae justa sunt facit omnibus, injustis ac malignis, et omnes benignantur in operibus ejus. Et non est in judicio ejus iniquum, sed fortitudo, et regnum, et potestas, et majestas omnium aevorum.

Lib: Tert: Esdrae. Cap IV, 38–40.

Preface

THIS BOOK had its origins in a paper I prepared for the meeting of the British Association at Manchester in 1962. I had been asked to speak to the educational section of the Association on the teaching of history, and thinking matters over it seemed to me that it would be of advantage to suggest that a most important use of historical education might well be the training of young people, whether they intend to specialize in historical studies or no, in the application of the methods of historical scholarship as an antiseptic. What I meant was this. Every man or woman is confronted with a great deal of history every day of their lives. They read recent history in their daily newspaper; the problems they have to confront have been provided by history; history in one form or another suggests the data for their opinions, informs their language and colours their ideas. However, much of the history they use is for one reason or another untrustworthy. Some of it was never systematically learnt, some is only hazily remembered, some of it has been definitely slanted for the purposes of propaganda. Yet however untrustworthy it may exert great power over their minds. Therefore it seemed to me that a valuable boon could be conferred on all people of reasonable intelligence if some prophylactic could be provided against the dangers which bad history, or the abuse of history, can create. This I believed could be done by training them in the criticism of history, largely by introducing them to the methods which historical scholarship has developed in the last one and a half centuries.

It was on these lines I composed my address to the British Association. I repeated it next year in much the same form at a conference of the Association of Teachers in Colleges and Departments of Education and afterwards elsewhere; my audiences being mainly school teachers, or teachers and students in training colleges. As I repeated what I had to say and attended to the discussions which followed I felt increasingly convinced of the importance of my theme, however faulty was my execution of it, and I became anxious to turn it into a book. This is the result.

As I suppose was inevitable the book is longer and more complicated than I had conceived it would be, and I have had to deal with problems which were not apparent to me when the paper was written. Nevertheless my intention is unchanged. The book is still an attempt to suggest ways of criticism which may afford some protection to the ordinary man or woman when they are confronted with statements about history. It is intended that it should do that and nothing more. It is not intended that it should supply a new philosophy of history, or to discuss such philosophies as exist. It is not intended to raise the question whether general laws are discernible in history, or what is the importance of historicism in human thought. It is not even intended to ask the question 'What is history?' These matters I leave to others, and I hope the restrictions on my intention will be respected by those who may wish to criticize the book. I myself am convinced that my limited objective is of great importance, and I hope that if I have failed to attain it someone else will do the work more effectively.

I have to thank Miss Helen Simpson and Professor Arnold Lloyd for the encouragement which led me to convert my paper into a book. Dr G. R. Elton, Professor Christopher Cheney, Professor Walter Ullmann and Mr Peter Laslett have helped me on a variety of points. Professor Wallace Davies of Philadelphia tracked down for me the evidence produced before a sub-committee of the Senate of the United States on the alteration of a tape from a tape recorder, which I had originally learnt about from an allusion to Alan Barth, *The Price of Liberty* (New York, 1961). In my search for light on the history of shorthand and the related problems connected with the reporting and editing which lie behind the *State Trials* I was much helped by Sir John Neale, Professors M. C. Bradbrook and G. W. Keeton and Dr A. J. Gurr. On the question of quantification I owe much to articles sent to me by Professor W. O. Aydelotte; one useful example was given me by Dr F. A. Stubbings and Mr F. H. Sandbach and help on another by Professor H. Chadwick. To all these scholars I owe great gratitude for the readiness with which they put their learning at my service. I alone am responsible for the use made of it.

I owe my thanks to Mr F. A. Simpson for allowing me to use his important article on Lytton Strachey's treatment of Cardinal Manning, and to Dr R. Robson for his kindness in reading the whole book in typescript and also in proof.

G. KITSON CLARK

Trinity College, Cambridge
25 May 1966

The Critical Historian

Note
Where in the footnotes reference is made to a work, which has been cited already, the page reference *within* the square bracket refers to the page in *this* book on which the first citation is made.

1

What Shall be Called 'History'?

HISTORY IS the record of what has happened in the past, of anything that has ever happened in the past, however long ago or however recently. It is sometimes suggested that what seems to be trivial is 'unworthy of the dignity of history', or that the account of what happened in the last few years 'cannot yet be called history'. In fact there is a tendency to confine the word 'history' to what can be put into a serious history book, and perhaps taught with safety and without controversial overtones in schools and colleges. It is a tendency much to be deplored. It is better to accept, as an axiom, the definition that any attempt to describe what has happened before the actual moment of narration shall be called history, for that carries with it the corollary that every such attempt presents some of the problems which are common to all historical work, and therefore may be subjected to the same critical technique as that to which history books are subjected.

Of course when the subject matter concerns very recent events it may not be easy to use this technique, and if the matter is trivial it may not be worthwhile. A rigorous examination of minor fancies about the past may seem rather ponderous and ridiculous. On the other hand a trivial detail does sometimes turn out to be important, and, even when there is no chance of that, there are those who find that a triviality becomes more amusing if it has some provable connection with something that once really existed or took place. That is however a matter of taste. What is not a matter of taste but one of necessity is that the technique of historical criticism should be applied to any account of matters that have occurred in the past to which any importance is attached.

Certainly what has happened very recently may present

unusual difficulties to the historian, or, to speak more accurately, the usual difficulties operating with unusual force. For instance it is very likely that a good deal of the information which seems to be essential to the proper interpretation of contemporary events will not be forthcoming, and that much of the information that is available can only come from obviously interested and probably unreliable sources. These things are, however, also in some measure true of all events in the past. Indeed it is always the first task of an historian to review any narrative to find what links are missing altogether, what parts depend on the mere assertion of a commentator and what parts, though apparently backed by evidence, are in fact only supported by matter which is inconclusive or suspect. Where what is defective cannot be supplied by further research it is an historian's duty to draw attention to the fact, so that men can know where they stand. These critical duties do not cease to be relevant because the subject matter is something which happened yesterday: on the contrary, if in such a case the gaps in the evidence are unusually wide and much of what exists comes patently from partizan sources, they become more important.

There are, however, those who feel that the passions excited by contemporary events are so strong and the immediacy of contemporary interests is so pressing that no one can be trusted to handle them with any semblance of impartiality. They think therefore that the title of *history* should be denied to the account of anything that happened within the last 20 or 30 years, because that title may only be given to what has been written objectively by the uncommitted. Those who believe this exaggerate the ease with which objective judgements can be made about any period of history. A glance at the problems of any century since 1500, and probably before that, should undeceive them. Many of the passions and prejudices which darken the mind today did not begin yesterday; they strike back through the centuries to imperil judgements about whatever events they touch. There are some conflicts which since they began have never been cold. There is for instance the conflict between the Churches which started at the Reformation. There are clashes between continuously opposed nationalities. There is the struggle between proletarian and bourgeois. There is the conflict between the historic entity which is now nicknamed the 'establishment' and the forces which attack it, which reaches at least as far back as the old assault on aristocratic government at the time of the French Revolution. Furthermore some of these modern quarrels have been artificially projected back into the study of remote periods to which they have no relevance, as in the absurd controversies which have sometimes developed between patriotic archaeologists of different nationalities about the relative levels of civilization of the primitive communities which once were situated in their respective territories. Or if public controversies do not intrude themselves to upset the balance there may be private controversies and rivalries, or professional preoccupations, such as the desire of a scholar to promote a theory of his own devizing or to destroy one that has been promoted by a rival; and, as if these sources of trouble were not enough, scholars have sometimes been known to develop irrational predilections for one dead individual or departed race and an equally irrational dislike for another.

In fact the distortions produced by bias are potentially present in any attempt to write history. Sometimes the danger is obvious and menacing, sometimes it is covert, coming from unexpected angles and in not easily detected forms. No historian should deny the probability of its presence in himself, or in any work or evidence which he is going to use. If he disregards this probability he will be the less able to control it. Of course it is most important, and may be most difficult, to control bias when it is the result of passion excited by issues which are still alive and still dangerous. But this may be as true of the history of what took place in past centuries as it is true of the history that appears in the morning paper.

2

The Dangers of History and their Cure

FOR THESE reasons it seems to be important not to deny the name of history to the records of any events however recent. So defined, history is a commodity in almost universal use. Gossip which makes any attempt to describe something which really took place must be called history. All business transactions depend on some form of history; so do all cases at law. All scientific results must depend on a rather specialized form of history. All journalism is an attempt to write history. Politics and the affairs of state cannot be understood without a knowledge of the immediate history of the transactions which are going forward, of the situation from which those transactions emerged and of the historical background before which all is enacted.

Indeed it is because of the importance of this background that the influence of history is so pervasive, and historians have such great opportunities to do good or evil. How pervasive this historical background is may perhaps be best realized through the way it affects the meaning, and colour, of words in common use. Take two words which might easily affect the same important modern argument, *barbarism* and *colonialism*. Each implies an epitome of past history, each possibly an explanation of it, each perhaps a generalization about it. *Barbarism* summarizes the mode of life which it is believed has characterized primitive nations, *Colonialism* the aggressive policy which it is said has too often been followed by more advanced ones. A variety of explanations are possible both of the mode of life of the one group and of the policy of the other. Each depends upon a particular reading of history. It may be held that barbarians have behaved barbarously because this was inherent in the stock from which they sprang, or alternatively that they happened to be situated away from the highway of human progress and had no chance to do otherwise. It may be held that colonialist annexation was a natural, in some cases a defensible, even in some cases an unavoidable, policy for the colonialist powers at certain epochs in the world's history; or alternatively that it was always an aberration to which the colonialist powers were driven either by something that was inherently evil in their nature, or by the ambition and greed of their ruling classes.

As men's interpretations of history differ so will their views about what policy should be followed in future. If barbarous nations have been barbarous because it was their nature so to be, then, if they become independent, they will slowly or quickly sink back into barbarism, and it is no good acting on the assumption that they will do anything else. If their barbarism was the result of historic chance then they are likely to be capable of moving forward with reasonable speed into a full independent civilized life. If the occupation of the territory by the colonial power was wholly indefensible, the wicked work of evil men, then perhaps everything that springs from it must be eliminated. If, however, the occupation was a natural phase through which both nations passed, and the motives of those to whom it gave control were possibly good, or partly good, then the colony may have inherited from it much that it will do well to keep when the connection has come to an end.

All this can be implied by the use of these words, and all of it, interpretations and conclusions, implies the making of a number of generalizations about difficult and often little known history. Even the use of the words at all implies fairly wide historical assumptions, for the different actions which are labelled with the words *barbarism* and *colonialism* may be so various that they cannot properly be grouped under one term, and the sense and implications of either word may be wholly misleading with regard to some of them.

Even when a word is more exact in its meaning, when it is in fact a term of art drawn from an abstract argument, it may have overtones which come from assumptions about history, and it is quite likely that it is these overtones which determine the force of its emotional impact. The word *capitalism* can no doubt be defined in the terms of reasonably strict economic analysis, yet it gains its colour very largely from what people believe capitalist society has been like. Or alternatively the words *communism* or *socialism* are words which strictly used should stand for various theories of the way in which society should be organized, but they are constantly used by people who have only the vaguest knowledge of the theories in question, but believe that they know, for good or ill, how socialists or communists have behaved. It is on that knowledge that their emotional reactions to the words are based.

If this is true of words which stand for abstractions it is likely to be still more true of the names of the great historic entities which have come down through a longer and more varied past. The words *German, Catholic* and *Jew* stand respectively for a nation, a Church and a race. They are used to describe things which exist in the world today, and therefore men's reaction to them should presumably be conditioned by what they are now. In fact, however, in each case men's reactions are largely affected by memories of history, or what passes for history, which seems to disclose the nature of Germans, or Jews, or Roman Catholics in their actions. As the selections of history which different people remember and the versions of history which different people accept will be by no means the same so their reactions to them will differ, sometimes very violently.

Sometimes a quite ordinary word will be caught up into the current of history and receive a new significance. A good example of this is the word *appeasement*. Its dictionary meanings are colourless, but in the years immediately before 1939 it became attached to a particular policy, and gained a new meaning in the vocabulary of politics which can cause strong emotional reactions. Others gain a colour from having served as the jargon of past controversies and so come to seem to have a clearer meaning than on analysis they possess; such words for instance as *Aryan, decadent* and possibly *reactionary*.

Yet though all these words gain their power from their association from history it is not necessary that the history which gives this power should have ever been systematically studied, or be very clearly remembered by those who are influenced by them. Some of their associations may have been derived from confusedly remembered lessons learnt at school, some inculcated by the reiterated assertions of politicians. Some associations survive from misty recollections of newspaper controversies, from scraps of special information or of personal experience, or the stories of chance acquaintances. The clear pictures of historical situations or of characters provided by historical novels or films, particularly those seen in youth, often seem to leave a curiously lasting impression. The reactions of a fair number of people in a past generation towards the Roman Catholic Church were probably, at least in part, affected by the novels of Charles Kingsley, possibly endorsed by a picture of the massacre of St Bartholomew drawn from the novels of Stanley Weyman. Yet, while on the one hand the entertainments of boyhood or girlhood seem sometimes to leave a deep impression, on the other, to an extent which is humiliating to schoolmasters and dons, the history which should have been learnt systematically in school or college seems often to have taken so little root that intelligent and apparently highly educated adults are curiously at the mercy of very questionable historical generalizations and descriptions against which any normal historical education should have guarded them.

From this haphazard mass of misty knowledge, scraps of information, fiction in fancy dress and hardly conscious historical memories is woven a network of historical associations which stretches over the whole field of human consciousness. Thus words are converted into spells, symbols are endowed with emotional force and stereotypes emerge which pretend to describe whole groups of people, and predict from their past their probable conduct in the future. Here in fact are some of the most powerful forces which control the human mind. They are of much use to those who wish to invoke irrational loyalties, they are also of great value to those who wish to use and to direct the emotion of hatred.

It is for this reason that the work of the historian can be turned into a propaganda weapon of great power. It can exhibit and enforce existing prejudices, and it can create new ones. Probably most people are more easily and more powerfully moved by the accounts of concrete events than by the rehearsal of abstract generalizations, and the historian can normally turn up suitable incidents and recount them vividly. Stories of

heroism, or stories of oppression, or best of all stories of martyr-
dom which combine the pathos of oppression and the glory of
heroism will make the heart beat faster and strongly enforce
the desired political or religious prejudices, particularly if
it is thought to be wrong to consider the case from the point of
view of the other side and right to forget the martyrdoms
which one's own friends may have inflicted on other people.

Behind this, endorsed by this concrete detail, is the picture
of the world which the historian may paint, portraying certain
nations and classes as being habitually in the wrong and working
evil, while other nations are immaculate, heroic and normally
their victims. Behind this again are the general theories of
human behaviour, which are held to determine the conditions
under which all life is lived for each of which, whatever they
are, the historian can usually supply conclusive evidence.

The influence of history may therefore be great, and may be
wholly evil. It can be used by the self-deceived or by the plain
liar, it can be used by the fanatic or by the propagandist, it
can excite passions which lead to hatred and so to human
violence and misery. It engenders the venom which makes
wars likely. How dangerous the abuses of misapplied history
may be the record of the last half-century in Europe, particularly in Germany, amply testifies, and, unless the human race
is unusually lucky, no doubt the record of the next half-
century, particularly in parts of Asia and of Africa, will
confirm.

Yet dangerous as these historical entanglements are it is not
easy to see a way of escape. A man cannot escape from history
by simply saying that he will disregard it, and will fix his eyes
firmly on the present. To disregard the past is very often the
surest means of becoming its slave. A man who ignores history
will still make the historical assumptions which are implicit in
most language and in all political judgements, but he will not
know he is making them and so will be unable to criticize
them or reconsider the evidence on which they are based.
Nor is it possible to escape the great historical controversies
which split politics and shake the world. If a man takes the
Olympian view, which attracts so many people, that there is
always much to be said for both sides in any controversy, and
that therefore the truth must lie about halfway between the

extremes, he will play himself straight into the hands of the least responsible of the contestants; for the more extravagant are the statements made the more certainly will the middle position be drawn to the side of those who make them. Nor is there a possible retreat into what purports to be a careless universal scepticism such as commends itself to the sophisticated. Such a scepticism is stupid because it is blind and can never be complete. A man must believe something, and the fact that he has summarily rejected a great many things which other people believe is no guarantee that he is able to criticize whatever it is that he himself accepts.

There is only one way to escape. It is laborious, frustrating and uncertain: but there is no alternative. What has to be done is not to disregard history, but to use it more effectively. Perhaps the first thing to be done is, as far as possible, to get clear in one's own mind what historical conclusions the language, the political creeds, the programmes and the propaganda of the moment assume. When this has been done clearly the next task should be to consider upon what evidence such conclusions must rest if they are to be believed and whether such evidence is likely to be available and to be reliable. All this may have a wholesome purgative effect. A certain number of the historical assumptions which are made by political propagandists or implied in common political jargon when clearly postulated can be seen to be not credible, or even if they are credible there can still be no reason to believe them for the evidence which would be needed to substantiate them could never be produced.

Such a negative result is of course valuable. If men have learnt to doubt what they ought to doubt clearly something valuable has been achieved. But as clearly it would be both frustrating and dangerous if that was all that could be done, if after the nonsense had been dissipated all that was left was so uncertain and evasive that no man could risk using it as a basis for his beliefs and calculations. There is a well known danger in being empty, swept and garnished. Every man needs some conception of the past upon which he can rely if he is to talk about the present or plan for the future, and if no clear conceptions are vouchsafed him by critical scholarship he will get them from elsewhere.

Fortunately there should be no need for him to do that. Great difficulties stand in the way of establishing the complete and unquestionable truth about anything, but it is seldom difficult to establish something nearer the truth than what is generally believed. Certainly the evidence is always more doubtful, or equivocal, or incomplete than is normally obvious to the casual observer, and it should be accepted as an axiom that motives are always a matter for speculation. Worst of all, all investigators are human and, being human, are liable to bias. Nevertheless against all this should be placed the positive achievements of historical scholarship particularly since the development of historical method began in the last century. Since then, indeed from long before then, historical scholars have tried to develop methods which will enable them to extract as much truth as possible from the evidence available and a tradition which will eliminate as far as possible the influence of personal bias from their work. In neither task have they been completely successful, nor can they be. In many important historical enquiries absolute certainty is not to be obtained, the evidence will not supply it; and bias of one sort or another is protean and all pervasive, no man is free from it. Nevertheless it can be said with some confidence that in very many matters the labours of scholars have produced a version of history which is a better guide to what really happened, a more secure basis for thought and action than those versions which usually confirm political credulity and supply material for propaganda.

Even so no version of history ought to be believed without question. No historian should be trusted implicitly. If it were possible it would be desirable to learn something of a historian's personality and preoccupations in order to be able to check his bias; that would however be often tedious and often impracticable, for the lives and personalities of many scholars are necessarily and properly lost in an unmemorable past. In all cases, however, the work should be considered critically in relation to the evidence which it purports to use, and if it is accepted it should be accepted tentatively not as something definitive, but as a workable hypothesis, which may be modified or replaced in due course by the further work of scholarship and the accumulation of new evidence.

To adopt this attitude, to effect these criticisms or even to know what criticisms might be relevant requires training. Much of it is not very difficult training. Much indeed consists in learning to ask of any report certain simple questions, the purport of which is obvious as soon as they are described. In addition to this it is probably desirable to study the methods of certain historians, sometimes to learn what should be done and sometimes to learn what should not be done and to be shewn the pitfalls into which may intelligent men have fallen. In most cases what has to be mastered are the obvious and easily forgotten lessons of commonsense. It is true that historians do use specialized techniques, but they can confidently be left to the specialists who use them, though it is interesting to know of their existence. But though this training in historical criticism should not be difficult it is suggested that it might give to any man or woman who has received it something of great value, the realization of how much, or how little, they can expect to know about matters of importance and possibly the capacity to criticize the evidence on which the dangerous legends or myths of the world may be supposed to be founded, or at least to see how it might be criticized.

If there is truth in this it would seem to be important that the habits of historical criticism should be developed from the moment anyone begins to take an intelligent interest in history, or for that matter in current affairs. This means that children should be introduced to the study in their later years at school, particularly those children who are specializing in history, but not only those children since these techniques are for general use. This would be incompatible with the dogmatic way in which in the past history used too often to be taught. Sometimes, even in the not too remote past, the facts of history, neatly tabulated with their causes carefully enumerated, were rationed out to those whose privilege it was to learn but not to argue, to be accepted because the teacher said so or because they were to be found in that authoritative oracle 'the book', whatever book it was that the school was using or examiners had prescribed. It was a method which never satisfied the best teachers, and, it may be guessed, is very little used now. Nowadays there is freer discussion of historical issues, a much greater use of original material, and it is suggested that there might be a wider discussion of the problems presented by the use of evidence both by the historians who write history books and the historians who write for the daily newspaper.

It is for this reason I wish to turn in my next chapters to some of the problems presented by the criticism of historical work. It may be well to start by comparing the work of the historian with the work of two other groups engaged in expert enquiries, the lawyers and the natural scientists, and then to discuss the historian's relationship to his own task.

3

History and the Law Courts: Two Standards of Proof

IT MUST be admitted that at first taste historical criticism may seem to be as disagreeable as an old fashioned medicine. Its results are less likely to add to man's knowledge of the past than to demonstrate that of the things about the past, which he thinks he does know, some are doubtful, some impossible. No doubt this is useful; it is antiseptic. If historical legends and fantasies help to feed the hatred of the world then it is as well to send them down the drain. But the action is not likely to be a popular one. When men and women are emotionally committed to an account of an event which endorses their dearest animosities they do not relish being told that it could not have happened as they say, and quite possibly never happened at all. Even in quite trivial matters they do not much like the stories which they have always enjoyed telling being probed and probably discredited by a silly pedant in the name of historical truth. The exercise seems to them to be unnecessary and probably the result of academic conceit. It seems so little worth while to sacrifice much that is exciting, or amusing, or picturesque in order to gain in exchange for it what is dull and indecisive, and in many cases to learn no more than how little it is possible to know.

Yet, even were the results as uniformly devastating and dreary as they are often painful, the work of searching and cleaning the wounds of history would have to go on. In fact, however, there are mitigations. The human beings and events which emerge from rigorous historical enquiry and after severe historical criticism are often stranger, more idiosyncratic and in reality more interesting than what is normally supplied by the commonplaces of romanticism, or of political partisanship, for they have been quarried from the hard deposit of unpredictable fact that lies behind and gives strength to, the writing of all real history, and are not simply compacted of prejudices of which we already know too much.

Fortunately, also, the actual process of search into this body of fact in itself attracts a good many people. Apart from anything else many people conceal within themselves an eager amateur detective anxious to make discoveries which the professionals have missed, and the problems of detection provided by history present opportunities not offered by the detective stories of fiction. The problems of history have not been solved already. The clues have not been planted by a skilful hand to be gathered together in the last chapters to support a conclusion which surprises everyone but the author. It is quite likely that many of the clues which may help an historical enquiry are as yet known to no man, and when they do turn up no one will fail to be surprised at what they suggest.

There is, however, one disadvantage to be set against this. These are stories which may have no last chapters. In a detective story the enquiry leads inevitably to the identification of the guilty party, and when all is over there will be the final exposition by the master detective to show how all the clues in fact led inevitably to this result. The historical researcher may achieve no decisive result in a lifetime's research. All that may be vouchsafed may be an hypothetical conclusion veiled and swathed by those tiresome and frustrating words 'probably' and 'perhaps'. If one of the detectives did attempt a disquisition on such clues as are available he might only be able to show no more than that they might lead equally well to one of several incompatible conclusions, and even so his brother detectives might not agree with him.

The primary reason for this contrast is of course the fact that the writer of a detective story must as a matter of professional necessity reach a decisive result. His clues are planted to be discovered, and they must in the end support a line of argument which is complete, or apparently complete. There is, however, another fact about the detective story writer which is worth consideration. He does not have to prove his results.

When the hunt in a detective story has come up with its quarry and the handcuffs have been fitted to the right wrists, it is sometimes an amusing exercise to consider how much of what the detective has asserted could possibly be established in court under the conditions the law prescribes, whether in fact the dramatic arrest would be at all likely to be followed by a conviction. A certain doubt on this point in the minds of the writers of these stories seems to be suggested by the frequency of the occasions on which the villain is made to betray himself at the end by self-condemning attempts at flight or violence, or by a convenient suicide leaving an ample confession. An historian cannot precipitate these decisive finales. He must endeavour to try to prove his conclusions as decisively as possible, and it is therefore important for him to consider carefully the tests which a law court might apply to his methods of proof.

This does not mean that the work of a law court and that of an historical enquiry are exactly parallel. They are not, for they have slightly different objectives. It is the object of an historian to get as near to the truth about people and events in the past as he can. That is, however, not the primary object of a law court: its object must be to come to a decision, a decision which must as far as possible correspond with the realities of the case, but also a decision which must be fitted into those categories which the general framework of the law supplies, and on which action can be taken. Problematical conclusions, or conclusions which are irrelevant to the restricted purposes of the law, are of no use.

This restriction is of great importance in a criminal trial. In a criminal trial only two possible decisions can matter, guilty or not guilty; probably guilty or possibly guilty, probably innocent or possibly innocent, can all of them only mean one thing, not guilty. Therefore in a criminal trial artificial rules are introduced to prevent a man from being convicted if he has not been proved to be guilty in the eyes of the law, even if the balance of probability is against him. For this reason evidence is automatically excluded which an independent enquirer, anxious only to establish the truth, would have taken into account. Indeed in an English trial there is, in the interests of what is conceived to be fair play, the most remarkable restriction on the power of the court to uncover the truth. In most trials the person who is likely to know most about the subject matter of the trial is the accused person, and yet the accused person is not, at least in theory, compelled to answer any questions at all.

Nevertheless, in spite of this difference in aim, those who research into history, and those who use history, ought to consider very carefully the rules which a court of law imposes on the evidence brought before it: such rules as the exclusion of hearsay evidence, the need for corroboration, or the duty to hear both sides to a conflict. They ought to be considered if only that it may be realised how often historians cannot afford to observe them if they are to get any results at all. Much of the evidence used by historians is hearsay. Often there remains only one account of an historical transaction and there is no independent testimony, which can be used as a check. To make matters worse the only surviving account may well be that of an interested party, while those who were on the other side have left behind no explanation or defence of what they did, nor yet any record of their accusations against their opponents.

This does not mean that an historian may not have advantages which the lawyer cannot enjoy. He may for instance have the use of evidence which is more extensive and revealing than what is likely to be available to a lawyer, or acceptable to a court. In fact on many 19th century topics there is a very large network of private letters supplementing the great bulk of published documents and reports, and these with the aid of the odd diary can bring the researcher very close to the actions and the minds of the people about whom he is writing, much closer in all probability than could be done by a cross-examination in court, which of course an historian is not likely to be able to do. Apart from anything else a man is more likely to be unguarded and truthful in a letter written to an intimate friend, or for business purposes, than when he is in the witness box. As the subject matter goes further back in time the mass, and the comprehensiveness, of the evidence is likely to be less. Even so in any period that can reasonably be called modern it can be very great and even when the matter relates to quite an early period, and the evidence available is thin, the chance survival of a document or a group of documents may give the historian an insight into what happened which he would never have gained in a court of law.

Nevertheless the extent of the evidence which survives from any date that is past, however recent, is always to some extent a matter of chance. There will always be gaps in it. Sometimes they will be serious, sometimes they will not matter. Sometimes diligent research can partially fill them, sometimes they can never be filled, and very often an historian can only bridge them by trusting to hearsay evidence, or uncorroborated evidence or partisan evidence. It is worthwhile to reflect at times what strictures a lawyer would pass on such evidence and then to consider how much of the history we accept depends on what he would reject: how much of it comes from the uncorroborated evidence of one man, how much of it comes exclusively from one side to a historical conflict, from the Athenians not the Spartans, from the Romans not the Carthaginians, from the orthodox not the heretics. It is also worthwhile to try to work out what kind of testimony could support accounts which we normally accept as being literally true in every detail and in every word used.

The words reported on various important occasions in the Gospels present obvious examples of this type of problem. For instance who reported the words Christ used in the garden of Gethsemane when the three guardian apostles were asleep? Who reported His conversation with the woman who had come to draw water when His disciples had left Him by the well in Samaria? Upon whose evidence did the writer of the fourth Gospel rely for his account of the dialogue with Pilate on the first Good Friday? The Jews who had accused Jesus remained outside the Palace lest they should be defiled; what chance was there for an independent witness, also presumably a Jew, not only to have got into the Palace, but to have come near enough to Pilate and his prisoner to hear with any certainty what was said? On other much less momentous occasions there is often considerable doubt about what has been said even where there are a large number of attentive persons present; moreover a report often gets modified either through transmission from one person to another before it is written down or through a lapse of memory on the part of a principal witness. What then, is the chance of the words having got modified in the cases I have cited?[1]

There can now be no answers to any of these questions. That fact does not necessarily impugn the essential truth of what has been reported, it does not even make it impossible that what has been reported is absolutely accurate. But it does raise a point which must be considered if it is ever a question whether we possess a complete and unquestionable account of every action that took place, of every word that was said. This is however a type of problem which by no means only concerns the Gospels. History is full of records of words spoken and of actions reported for which the testimony is uncertain, or plainly insufficient; the same thing is true of much that one encounters in the ordinary business of life. It is sometimes of the greatest importance to recognize this fact, and a good way to do this is to remember the rules which, over many centuries, lawyers have worked out for the treatment of evidence. In an ordinary historical enquiry those rules ought not to be decisive, for the historian's object is different from that of a lawyer. But it is healthy to keep in mind the challenge they present.

If, however, it is useful to compare the problems of the historian with those of a lawyer it will, also, be worthwhile to compare problems of historical research with those of another form of enquiry, in which the standard of proof is reputed to be even more stringent than what is required in a Law Court.

---

[1] A good example of subsequent uncertainty about words spoken on a public occasion is the variety of the versions of the words attributed to Huxley in his famous rebuke to Bishop Wilberforce at the meeting of the British Association at Oxford in 1860.

4

History and the Natural Sciences

MOST PEOPLE probably believe that, except perhaps for the results of direct inspiration or revelation, the highest degree of accuracy and certainty that human beings can achieve is to be found in what is established by scientific research. Any statement such as this, however, must be qualified by the reflection that a good many different types of enquiry come under the general heading of 'science'. There is physics and chemistry; there is astronomy; there is geology; there are the biological sciences; there is psychology; there are archaeology and anthropology, and there is much of sociology. There may be a unity behind all this. There is certainly a considerable overlap between science and science. But the subject matter studied through the various sciences differs widely, the techniques they have to use necessarily vary in accordance with the type of evidence which they have to handle, and it may be possible that the accuracy, certainty and finality of their results may vary also.

Not that any true scientist would claim that absolute finality and certainty can be achieved in any science. One unavoidably fallible and limiting factor cannot be excluded from the work which is done even in the most exact sciences. It is the human intellect. The facts will not reveal themselves: any enquiry demands an enquirer. A man or woman is required to isolate and define the problems to be investigated, to frame the scientific concepts to be used, to postulate the theories to be tested. Some of those who have been able to do these things have been some of the most gifted and remarkable men and women of whom there is record, but they retained the limitations of men and women. None of them were immune from mistakes. None of them could see further than it was historically possible for them to see at the moment of working. None of them could claim that their conclusions were final: such claims are not made by scientists. Science advances by proposing an hypothesis, using it as long as the results of research are compatible with it, and then abandoning it for one which fits the facts better.

This conception of the expendable hypothesis could be of great value to historians if they were prepared to accept it as a way of accepting opinions about history, and at other points the analogy of the problems of scientific research can suggest matters of great interest to them. But if the word 'science' covers so many different types of systematic enquiry, particularly if anthropology and sociology are to be included under it, then it may be a little difficult to say where science stops and history begins. Certainly there has been a welcome invasion of the territory of history by scientists. The discoveries of the natural scientist have been made available for historical work. For instance scientific methods have made the dating of objects from the remote past much more accurate. More and more is being learnt about periodic changes in the climate in historic times. It is knowledge to be used with the greatest caution, for it is not easy to see how it fits in with the ordinary course of historical enquiry and it is the kind of knowledge which tends to excite to recklessness the less stable among those who like to theorize about history. But it offers possibilities. If it could be combined with increased knowledge about the impact of epidemic diseases and the effect of changes in diet it seems possible that much that is important and new could be learnt about the growth of populations and the development of societies. At the same time there has been an extension into historical studies of what might be called scientific methods. In the 19th century historians learnt to use documents much more systematically and critically. In the 20th they are beginning to learn to use statistics. When they have to deal with large groups of people, or of objects, or of events they are beginning to learn to count, instead of hazarding guesses and using the loose composite words which have been common in history books, and they are learning to use the various techniques which science can suggest to them for estimation and enquiry into large numbers of particular units.

Certainly in the enquiry into certain specific subjects—
changes in the size of population, the stages of economic
growth, the problems of prices and wage rates—there can be
no clear frontier between what can be called 'historical' and
what 'scientific', and scientific methods and techniques will
almost certainly be extended into more and more fields of
study. Indeed an historian's work can be legitimately criticized
when scientific discoveries and scientific techniques, like the
proper use of statistics, are not used when they could be used
and ought to be.

Unfortunately there is another side to all this. For much
more than a century scientific language, and what purport to
be scientific theories, have been energetically exploited by the
reckless and by the spurious when writing about history.
Rather dreadful examples of this can be found in the various
misapplications of the doctrine of evolution which multiplied
exceedingly in the last quarter of the last century, or in the
ugly nonsense men learnt to talk about race. Nowadays
psychology has probably taken the place of zoology or anthropology as the science most open to abuse. But there is also
prevalent a form of historical and sociological thought with no
simple scientific ancestry but with scientific pretensions, which
are fortified by the use of an elaborate, heavily Latinized,
technical vernacular in which statements can be dogmatically
and impressively made which are commonplace, or unprovable,
or frankly meaningless.

Much of this miasma can be dissipated by clear thought, the
use of simple English, and an insistence that assertions must be
supported by evidence which depends on other authority than
the mere word of the promulgator of the theory. But where the
scientific case seems more formidable the historian should
refer it back to disinterested professional scientists working in
the appropriate field. Where scientific words and concepts are
being used it is important to be certain that they are being
professionally used and not misapplied, as the idea of evolution
was misapplied. Where a particular scientific theory is being
adapted it is necessary to make sure that those who are doing
this really understand what the original theory meant and in
what conditions it was valid. Most important of all is it necessary
to remember that what claims to have the authority of science

ought to be endorsed by the rigours of scientific proof, other-wise it is mere assertion couched in technical terms.

However the analogy of the natural sciences raises a deeper and more difficult problem for the historian than any suggested by the legitimate use of scientific methods and techniques, or the illegitimate use of scientific jargon. It is this. Work in certain sciences is made possible by two facts. It is possible to isolate what is going to be the subject of study from what is irrelevant to the enquiry, and it is possible to make and repeat experiments upon it in controlled conditions. So important are these possibilities that there have been those who claimed that no subject can properly claim the authority of a 'science', if its nature does not permit them. If this is so there must be a great gulf fixed between the results of historical and of scientific thought. For in history it is difficult, and normally wrong, to isolate the factors at work and it is always impossible to repeat the experiments.

It is not possible for instance to take the months of June, July and August 1914 and cause the whole tragedy from the murder of the Austrian Archduke to the British declaration of war on Germany to be re-enacted in order that the causes of that war should be better understood. This limitation also prevents the isolation of significant material. A great many different factors seem to have conspired in 1914 to produce the final hideous result—the activities of the Serbian Secret Societies and their relation to the Serbian government, the policies of the governments in Austria, Russia and Germany and of the general staffs of the Austrian and German armies, the fears of France, the hesitations of Britain. Behind this were larger more general causes, the emergence and aspirations of the Slavs, the effects of nationalism in Germany and elsewhere, the results of the history of Europe from the defeat of Austria in 1866 and indeed from before that, possibly the results of economic rivalries and many other factors too numerous to mention and possibly too obscure to be noticed. Since the problem of what causes war is of the greatest importance to humanity it would be very desirable to determine which of all these factors were the operative ones without which that war would not have happened. But it cannot be done. An historian cannot do what a scientist might do, that is repeat the whole process after having abstracted one, or more, of the factors to see whether the result in such case would be the same. He cannot unscramble the eggs of history in order to make up his mind which of them spoiled the taste of the dish that had to be eaten.

As a matter of fact the conception that some factors were operative causes of the outbreak of war and some were not is misleading. A large number of factors operating on each other led to what happened in the fatal days of late July and early August 1914. They cannot be considered separately and arranged in an order of importance because they cannot be conceived separately. The nature of one factor was partly dictated by its relationship to another factor and can only be defined in terms of that relationship. The nationalism of the Slavs can only be understood in relationship to the general development of nationalism in 19th century Europe and an operative cause, and a result, of that development was the development of nationalism in Germany, which in turn affected the history of Slav nationalism and was affected by it. No nationalism can be understood without understanding the economic and social structure of the country in which it exists; while the economic and social structure of a country cannot be understood without understanding the form which nationalism takes in it, and the part it plays. All these factors are inter-dependent; they cannot be separated from one another; they create a complex situation which controls what happens and which can not be resolved into its component parts.

Moreover the factors which make up the complexity of an historical situation are always changing. The selection of human beings who may at any given moment control or influence human affairs is constantly being replaced by another selection. The social structure of various countries develops in various directions, sometimes very slowly, some-times quickly. The size of their populations vary. Their economic prosperity changes both in relation to their own past and relatively to other communities. The methods of produc-tion improve. The armaments which men use in fighting alter. The general opinions which control mankind and the spiritual forces prevalent at any given moment change shape, or drift away, like the clouds, and alongside of these obvious changes

a thousand thousand more subtle and less discernible movements are always taking place, each with its effect on the
human situation at that moment. Even the face of nature
changes. The climate changes, the coast-line changes, the
amounts of surviving open country and of woodland change.
There are also probably from time to time mysterious and
important mutations in the nature and virulence of the
infectious diseases which may both affect the mortality rates
of a community, and also the welfare and effectiveness of
those who survive.

The effects of these changes are not cancelled by apparent
survivals and recurrences. Where things appear to survive for
a long time they survive into a new world and the way in
which it differs from the old one must affect them. Where they
recur they recur into a world that has already changed.
Therefore an historical situation will not only be the complex
result of complex causes, it will also always be unique. It will
be the result of a concatenation of circumstances which has
never happened before and will never happen again.

The realization of this fact has led to a controversy on the
question whether any generalizations about history are
legitimate—particularly generalizations which carry over from
one period into another one, or about things which occur in
different periods. It is not necessary to discuss that question
here. It is sufficient to say that it must be possible to make
some generalizations about the various things which appear in
history and the various events which happen; if it were not so
it would be impossible to talk about them, for language
implies some identity between the objects discussed. Indeed if
it were not possible to generalize about historical matters
history would have little interest and no significance. The very
writing of history seems to shew that some generalization is
possible. On the other hand part of the significance of an
event or an action must come from the particular situation in
which it takes place, and the meaning of spoken words necessarily depends on the mind and situation of the speaker and
the effect which he wishes to produce on those who hear him
at the moment of speaking. If then each situation in history is
unique the significance of every event, or action, or recorded
speech, must be in some way unique also.

This conclusion leads to what is perhaps the most important principle of historical scholarship, the principle of the importance of context. It is necessary when considering any historical evidence to take account of the situation at the moment in time when the event it records happened, and also at the moment when it was recorded. To neglect the context of historical evidence is to misunderstand its meaning. That, indeed, is the mistake most often made by those who wish to use history to provide themselves with arguments, but who will not study it.

These considerations affect the comparison between the conclusions of the historian and those of the scientist. For instance both the interdependence of the factors which go to make up human history and the unique character of each historical situation cast doubts on the validity of the various attempts which have been made from time to time to form a general science of human affairs by which all history can be explained. For the conclusions of a science to be valid it would seem that there must be enough uniformity and regularity of behaviour in the subject matter studied to make systematic observation possible. The great variety of the factors influencing the course of human history, the impossibility of isolating the effects of one factor from the effects of all the others, the complexity and the fluidity of the result, and above all the fact that each historical situation differs from every other historical situation, seem to make it improbable that a general science of history could be satisfactory or useful.

Those who have attempted to frame such a science have tried to avoid these difficulties by simplifying things. They simplify what happens in one period of history so that it can be the more easily compared with what happens in another period of history, or else they simplify all history by assuming that one factor—the climate, the size of the population, the prevalent methods of production or of government—has had so predominant an influence over human affairs that all the others are derivative from it, or are negligible. They then frame their science of history in the terms of the laws which they believe govern that factor. But the initial assumption cannot possibly be proved and is often on general grounds unlikely to be true. In most cases in fact history seems to need a good deal of rather drastic trimming and prodding to make it seem to be even probable.

This, however, does not mean that the historian cannot study the material which he uses scientifically. Nor is such study prevented by the fact that he cannot repeat the processes at will. After all the processes studied in a good many sciences cannot be repeated at will; they are descriptive rather than experimental sciences. Astronomy is to a large extent a descriptive science, so is geology. There is, however, one branch of science which is closer to human history than astronomy and geology. It is medical science. In medicine different people in different environments are studied and what is common to them, or to a selection of them, is recorded and analysed. This makes generalization possible. A disease is a sequence of events which has been observed to recur with such regularity among human beings that once it has started it is known, within limits, how it will continue. It is true that the progress of human knowledge has in many cases revealed the cause, or one of the causes, of the sequence, and that processes which resemble it have been discovered which can be repeated in controlled conditions. But there are still diseases whose causes are unknown, and in the earlier stages of the development of medicine, before the microscope was developed or the ancillary sciences came into existence, there were many more. Even so the results of close observation of what happened, accurately recorded and systematically analysed, yielded information of the greatest value for mankind.

The analogy between the work of an historian and that of the descriptive sciences should therefore be reasonably close. The historian's first duty is careful and expert observation. Even if he cannot explain what happened or ascribe a cause to it, if he is able to use the evidence to get as near as is practicable to an accurate account of it he has performed an important service for mankind. But it is impossible to describe any series of events in human history without making some attempt at an explanation, and any explanation, whatever a man's philosophical view on the question of causation, must in effect present some hypothesis about the causes which made the sequence of events happen in the way it did. The historian may not be able to explain war in general, nor yet define what were the master causes of the war of 1914–18, but by describing carefully what were the events which led up to that war he can point to certain factors which played a part in starting it. If he does this as clearly and accurately as he can he will do something valuable. But he can do more. All positive work has its negative side. He can not only suggest what events probably led to the war, he can dissipate legends about the causes of the war which are based on no evidence, or are contrary to the evidence. All this can be done by the historian without involving himself in the discussion of any general theory about the way in which human beings or human societies behave. Since, however, the normal subject matter of history—wars, the operation of trade, the evolution and behaviour of nations, the development of governments—is also the subject matter of all theories about the way human affairs are conducted such theories must be based on his work. If they are not their generalizations are mere moonshine and fantasy, even if they are expressed in scientific terms, or what appear to be scientific terms.

A reasoned hypothesis based on a careful consideration of evidence which has been tested critically and systematically might be considered to have a claim to be called 'scientific'. Indeed it seems possible that much historical work has a better title to that question-begging adjective than much theorizing that assumes it as a matter of right. But it is important not to exaggerate here. Many descriptive sciences can provide much more exact and certain conclusions than can most historical research. The clear definition of their enquiries permits this. Those who are researching in them can exclude from their calculations adventitious and irrevelant factors; they can be sure that the repetitions on which their theories are based are exact repetitions. These things are not generally possible in history. It is probably possible for a geologist to be sure that he knows everything that led to the deposit of a stratum; it is not possible for an historian to feel any security that he knows everything that led to the development of a nation. It can be said with certainty that one eclipse of the sun is the exact repetition of another eclipse of the sun; it is not possible to be sure that one political revolution is the exact repetition of another political revolution. For this reason the results of any historical reasoning, except perhaps the highly specialized results of such studies as demography or the history of prices, must be more tentative and approximate than the results of the more exact observational sciences, and any generalization based on them less certain.

This not only affects the way in which it is legitimate to use the generalizations based on normal historical evidence, it also affects the treatment of that evidence, particularly when what is under consideration is what to reject as impossible. In many sciences it is possible to say that a law, say the second law of thermodynamics, which has been repeatedly confirmed by exact observations, is so certain that there is an overwhelming probability that any evidence which contradicts it is wrong. In general human affairs, except when the evidence contradicts very simple propositions, such as that a man cannot be in two places at the same time, or defy the laws of gravity, or take an active part in human affairs when he is dead, it is unlikely to be possible to impose a decisive negative test of this sort. What is often done, therefore, is to judge not by law but by analogy, that is to say that this sequence of events resembles another sequence of events so closely, and the report of something in the second sequence is so unlike anything in the first that it is probable this report is wrong. This is obviously a much more shaky argument. Nevertheless argument on these lines is continually used in the consideration of evidence both in historical research and in the ordinary business of life. It is very often the only argument that can be used, but it is important to realize on what very insecure foundations it often rests.

For if ordinary men and women have to make up their minds whether it is probable that an event which has been reported to them could have taken place they cannot compare it with what has been repeatedly recorded in a carefully observed sequence; they have to compare it with what experience and knowledge seem to show is the way things in general do happen in the world. If a series of events is reported which seems to be entirely unlike any other events, which they believe have been credibly reported at any other time, they will scrutinize the evidence for them with unusual care, and perhaps whatever the evidence in its favour, they will dismiss the report as being the result of mistake or fraud.

This is, after all, the argument that people normally use against there being any possible truth in stories of ghosts, or the supernatural, or paranormal. It is true that ghost stories often contain physical improbabilities, figures suddenly appearing in locked bedrooms or walking through brick walls; but given the premise on which ghost stories rest these things are not impossible. Many people, however, see no reason to accept that premise. They argue that there do not appear to be a sufficient number of adequately authenticated cases even of such paranormal events as cases of telepathy or phantasms of the living to force belief in events which are so different from the ordinary experience of life.

This is a favourite argument and it closely resembles the kind of test that most people, historians as well as others, apply all their lives both to descriptions of actions in which they are interested, and to any explanation of the motives of the actors involved. The questions: 'Is that action probable? Could it have happened like that?', or 'Does that motive ring true?' are very unconsciously translated in the mind into the questions: 'Does that action, as reported, remotely resemble any other actions of which I have reliable knowledge?', or 'Does the suggested motive correspond with human motives as I have known them in myself or other people?' Very often the whole process is more or less unconscious—only very simple people say, 'They never heard the like', and that possibly most often in works of fiction, but that sentiment is often the true meaning of more sophisticated expressions of disbelief. Certainly in the case of ghost stories the claim that this test has been consciously applied is often confidently made, and this is the more remarkable because the people who say with most assurance that they do not believe in the supernatural or paranormal because no authenticated accounts of supernatural or paranormal events exist have very often taken no trouble at all to find out whether or not this is true. If they did the evidence, which is easily available, might surprise them. For, leaving on one side the more melodramatic old-fashioned ghost stories, and possibly, in general, stories of phantasms of the dead, the amount of carefully checked evidence in favour of phenomena, which are to say the least of it paranormal—phantasms of the living, telepathy, clairvoyance and even possibly pre-cognition—which has been laboriously collected by the appropriate societies is impressive. If those who deny its authenticity had considered and rejected this evidence their position would be defensible; but in fact many of them have not looked at it, and have no intention of doing so.

It is not within the purpose of this book to consider what effect a review of this evidence might have upon their opinions. The point of importance here is that in this case a preconceived prejudice is masquerading as the result of a systematic enquiry. The same type of self deception often occurs when people say that something is against the 'laws of nature' without saying clearly what 'law' has been contravened. Most often, however, the test of probability is in fact applied unconsciously. Men and women constantly judge what they consider to be probable by tests which they use naturally and automatically without knowing clearly what they are doing, or why they are doing it.

Probably the best way to understand this process is to try to realize what touchstones one uses oneself when one has to judge what is probable or possible. If one is honest with oneself it will I think be clear that they are provided by a curious assortment of mental bric-a-brac which has been collected at different times in life. There is one's own personal experience sometimes consciously remembered, sometimes wholly or partially forgotten, but none the less powerful for that. There are the experiences, and the prejudices, of the groups with which one has passed one's life. There is the knowledge of the world one has acquired by reading, possibly by reading straightforward descriptions of things and events, possibly by reading fiction. There may be some sort of philosophy which claims to explain what the world is like, and there are likely to be life-long prejudices pretending to be a philosophy. No doubt behind these things there will lurk deep-seated psychological factors of which one is unconscious. Yet though the mass of factors which influence one's sense of what is probable may be very heterogeneous, there is one thing common to them all. They are all in some way peculiar to oneself. What may present itself as the commonsense judgement of all sensible men may very well be heavily coloured by what is in one's own mind and no one else's.

This is a point of very considerable importance. For if a

man's personal experience has been narrow, particularly if it has not extended by reading or by a natural interest in other people, the danger is that this sense of what is probable will be unduly narrowed also, that he will refuse to credit situations which are entirely remote from his mode of life and cut down the personalities he meets to patterns which fit in with what he thinks he knows. Even when a man's experience has been wide he may find it difficult to believe in a personality which has been formed by an environment completely different from his own. Even so Neville Chamberlain tragically failed to see the dangerous potentialities of Hitler; even so F. D. Roosevelt could not recognize the differences between himself and Stalin.

It is for this reason that it is valuable to read history to make the acquaintance of men formed by very different environments, but the same consideration may suggest that it is impossible to write history. For if men fail to understand contemporaries whom they can meet how can they hope to understand men who have been dead for centuries? The answer to that question is personal and can only be considered in connection with the relationship of the historian to his own work.

5

History and the Historian

IF THE truths of science require a scientist to discover them, history requires an historian to write it. If we look back into the past what we see is not just what happens to be there but what has been selected and displayed for us by other human beings. Any student can test that fact by examining his own picture of history and then considering what parts of it he owes to other historians; in English history for instance I recognize what I owe, to name the recent dead, to Sir Lewis Namier, to R. H. Tawney, to G. M. Trevelyan, to C. H. McIlwain or E. Halévy, or to go a little further back to Alfred Pollard, to Maitland and to a varied body of men and women who have written on the medieval constitution from Bishop Stubbs onwards, and in the history of affairs outside Britain to a much larger body of historians, some European and some American. The work of some of these scholars may have been criticized, but if a man is honest with himself he will realize how much of what he sees he still sees with their eyes and because they shewed it to him in the form in which it appeared to them.

This relationship is not confined to those who are consciously studying history, or who know what dead historians have done for them. Anyone who has some conception of the past, and it is difficult to imagine a man or woman who has none, is likely to have gained a large part of his conception from the descriptions, reconstructions or generalizations of other people. He may not know upon whom he is relying, indeed if he knew who it was he might not be best pleased. It is sometimes interesting to calculate how much of Karl Marx's analysis of both history and society is used by people who are rather emphatically not marxists. The old Whig conception of English history which had its culmination in the work of Hallam and Macaulay has been dead and discredited for many years, but its ghost still power-fully haunts the minds of Englishmen. Even when men have formally rejected the source from which an historical picture has been derived the picture itself may linger on. Whatever his beliefs may be everyone who has received the European tradi-tion in any form has gained much from the often nameless historians who contributed to the Bible.

In all these cases whether it has been consciously accepted or unconsciously assumed the view of the past which men have become used to and on which they have acted has been the creation of other human beings. The facts may seem to speak for themselves, but they always require a human being to give them utterance, and a number of essentially personal judgements on the part of someone is likely to have influenced what they say. In some cases this is obvious. In a later chapter it will be necessary to criticize some work of Macaulay since it relates to some records that are relevant to the argument. But Macaulay is an easy target. He was a great historian. The imaginative force which he applied to his *History* makes it one of the most remarkable pieces of historical writing in English and a lasting contribution to our perception of British History in the late 17th century. But he was eclectic, undiscriminating and at times inaccurate in his use of evidence, and his prejudices are obvious. There is therefore no need to emphasize the fact that Macaulay's personality and opinions affected all the history he wrote. It is more difficult to remember that the same thing is true of any man or woman who has ever written about the past. The most severely analytical history based, as it would seem, directly on statistics by a bloodless scholar who seems to be troubled by no bias and no human feeling is nevertheless the result of a series of decisions in the selection and presentation of evidence and in the deductions to be drawn from it which must be affected by the personality and pre-delictions of the author. Even the way in which a graph has been plotted and presented will be controlled by the ideas of the man who drew it up. And where the agency of any human being is involved then his passions, his interests, his scale of values, his own particular view of the universe, will affect the result.

It is impossible for the ordinary user of history to escape this fact. He can only see the past as it has been presented to him by other people. But it is desirable for him to be aware of this condition, and to give some thought to the way in which the personality of a historian is likely to have affected what has been received from him. Nor is it only the personality of the historians who have worked for us which will affect our view of the past. In fact some part of it will have come from historians of past ages whose whole approach to history was different from our own, a fact which will certainly have affected the legacy we have received from them.

For instance we have probably all received from what may be called early historians, not only the historians of the Bible but the historians of Greece and Rome and other ancient civilizations and also of the Middle Ages, and in order to understand what we have received from them it is necessary to think oneself back into the period in which the history was recorded. It may have been a world in which the accurate dating of events which were at all remote was difficult or impossible and the perspectives of the past were not pegged as firmly and as accurately as they are for us. It is likely to have been a world in which the conventions in the presentation of history, particularly in the use of direct speech, was not ours and in which indeed the whole conception of the past was different from our own. Before the 18th century the conception of progress or process which consciously or unconsciously plays a great part in modern thought is likely to have been absent, and at different dates very different conceptions of the course of history would have been assumed by historians. To some ages it would appear to be static, the same kind of events in the same kind of conditions repeating themselves in generation after generation without noticeable change or much significance; to some it would appear cyclical, to some tragic, the story of moral commitments working out their inevitable consequences, and to some the stage in which a divine plan was demonstrated and events had their prophetic significance and were probably prefigurations of what was to come or types or symbols of something which had happened. But whatever view of the course of history was accepted it must necessarily have affected what men wrote about it.

An important change in the writing of history comes with

the Renaissance, but this change did not introduce a uniform style of history or a view of the past which has lasted to this day. The 16th and 17th century historians, and the view of the past which was held in the 16th and 17th century, were different from those of the 18th century and those who were essentially of the 18th century differed from the romantic historians of the early 19th century, the romantic historians from the more scientific historians of the later 19th century, and so on. Yet it is probable that the ordinary educated man, and probably the ordinary uneducated man also, has inherited something from every stage in the development of the writings of history, and what he has inherited is likely to be moulded by the preconceptions of the era in which it was produced. It is important to be aware of this. It is not to be expected that ordinary preoccupied men and women will have the time to study the history of historiography, fascinating and relevant though that history is. But it is important that they should at the least realize that these differences of background and attitude have existed, in order that they may be able to evaluate the historical assumptions which persist in their own minds.

What they may have received from a remote past will not, however, present them with their most difficult and important critical problems. There is another form of history, usually anonymous, often vague and evasive, which it is most desirable to bring under critical review. This is the history which is assumed as a matter of course by journalists, by politicians and indeed in ordinary conversation. Very often much of this has been repeated so often that people are inclined to accept it as self-evident fact. But in reality every statement about what has happened in the past has had an author, someone who observed it, recorded it, repeated it, and every author is subject to the limitations and defects of humanity. It will be difficult to diagnose these defects when you do not know who he was, but it is as well to recognize that they may have been there. It is therefore as well to try to trace where possible any fact back to a source which can be checked; if it is a quotation to the original context in which it appeared, if it is an event to a description by a named author whose statements can be tested. Even if the historical knowledge with which one is concerned comes in the ordinary way from a recognized history book it is still, as far as this is possible, desirable to find out something about the author, about his methods, his reputation, his possible bias.

Before these questions are considered, however, there is another to be asked of any history book. Is one dealing with the historian who did the work on which it rests, or has an intermediary stepped in? Various types of intermediary are possible. There is the historian who simply repeats the statements of other historians with, or very probably without, acknowledgement. There is the historian who thinks for himself but bases his thought entirely on the facts supplied by other historians, and the type of writer upon whom school teachers too often have to depend, the textbook writer who serves up historical work for the young. In each case it is probable that there will be some distortion, either wilful distortion, which is in most cases unlikely, or distortion through ignorance and carelessness, which is more likely, or else distortion through abbreviation, which is the most usual form of distortion. Anyone who has taken the trouble to compare a textbook with the historical works it epitomizes can realize how devastating the results of this distortion can be—how stark and meaningless a fact can be without the background which should explain it, how peremptory and dogmatic a statement becomes without the argument by which the author originally justified it, or how misleading a quotation can be which has been bandied from hand to hand until it is infinitely removed from its original context, and has probably lost some of its most significant words. But most depressing of all is the gradual degradation of an historical theory as it becomes detached from its originator's carefully considered and guarded words and reappears first in a popularized version, then in notes dictated in class and then comes to rest at last, in dreadful caricature, in the answer to a question in a school examination paper.

A first step in historical criticism therefore is to try to reach back to the original writers, to the historians that is who thought the thoughts and did the research, whose results are daily being served up as pemmican. A second step may well be to try to see how the work was done. For this reason there is virtue for teachers, and for reasonably adult learners, in using books which possess some learned apparatus: footnotes with references, bibliographies and a discussion of sources. This is not to say that the multiplicity of footnotes, or the length of bibliographies necessarily supply secure guarantee that the book is reliable. These things can be the most effective instruments of deception. But their existence is a tribute to the fact that history must be based on evidence and the study of them may show how the work is done.

For the same reasons it may be well to look at some parts of some of the great historical controversies, though seen as a whole these often become tedious and reiterative. A most useful type of book is one which takes one historical issue and shows how it has been treated by different historians at different periods. There are two outstanding examples of books of this sort: A. Schweitzer, *The Quest of the Historical Jesus*, and Pieter Geyl, *Napoleon: For and Against*. They are useful in this context not so much because of their bearing on the particular subject under discussion but because they demonstrate clearly how differently the same facts can be interpreted by different historians writing in good faith, and particularly how different are likely to be the interpretations of historians writing at different dates.

For it must always be remembered that history is after all the reflections of a man or woman working at one point in time on what happened at another point in time, and in considering the result the date at which the history is being written is as much to be taken into account as the date of the events which are being written about. As I have already mentioned him it may be convenient to take Macaulay again as an example. As has been said there were certain defects in his vision. He did not understand the Puritans, about whom he was inclined to be abusive. He was stupid and uncomprehending about Laud. He could not see what Cranmer's problem was. There were many things in the economic problems which confronted both the earlier and the later Stuarts which he failed to grasp. These failures were partly temperamental. Macaulay's religion, though perfectly sincere, was inclined to be a sensible man's religion, which did not leave much room for exaltation and mysticism, and he could not really understand exaltation and mysticism in other people. In addition to this Macaulay did not possess knowledge which comes to us easily enough because we have the advantage of the century of historical research which has succeeded his death, and lastly, he was blinded by the fact that he was an optimistic, self-confident, whig of the first half of the 19th century and there were certain attitudes which were fairly common in the 17th century which he could not share. We know better nowadays, at least we know better in some things. There is little doubt that in others Macaulay is much nearer a moderate 17th century, or early 18th century, whig than is anyone alive today, and therefore he is likely to understand the things he shares with the 17th century much better than we can understand them, who do not share them.

In fact criticism by someone writing in the mid-20th century, of an historian, who wrote in the mid-19th century, about events in the 17th century is necessarily a three-point relationship, in which the vision of both the historian and the critic has been affected by the flux of time. For the flux of time affects the whole of a man's vision: it affects his sympathies, it affects his values, and it also affects, what was spoken of earlier, his sense of the probable, his sense of the things which he believes could happen in the world, and of the things which he believes to be impossible. An obvious example of this is the belief in miracles. An historian of the 14th century could accept the evidence for a near contemporary miracle without trouble. After the beginning of the 18th century many historians, and, after the beginning of the 19th century, most historians would reject the account of any miracle, except perhaps a biblical one, out of hand, unless perhaps they were Roman Catholics.

Even more generally important is the fact that the flux of time also affects the motives which historians are prepared to credit to the people about whom they write. Romantic historians in the early 19th century were inclined to credit a good many of the actors in history with exalted and extravagant motives, good and bad. In much of the 19th century rather markedly virtuous motives were often attributed to people whom the record favoured. In the 20th century such motives are likely to be suspect, particularly if they smack of patriotism, or Christian devotion. On the whole a flatter, drabber, sometimes more cynical, view of the human personality is more acceptable. On the other hand rather elaborate psychological explanations are likely to be believed even when they are based upon curiously little of the kind of evidence which is usually considered to be necessary to establish the assertions of those who are not psychologists.

What has however been said about historians is to say no more than that the most careful and scholarly historians are all of them men and women writing at a particular date, entertaining particular opinions and using particular methods in handling their material and that if their work is to be used with confidence it is necessary to know the way in which these factors which are personal to themselves have affected it. This however is true of anyone who has written anything on any topic. It is certainly as true of the man who writes about matters which are for him in the present, or nearly in the present, as it is true of the man who writes about things which are certainly in the past. The advantage which the professional historian presents to the critic is that by the rules of his craft he must attempt to shew by what means he reached his conclusions and what evidence he used. It is not normal, indeed it would not in many cases be possible, for a journalist to do this. Nevertheless the problems of a journalist and an historian are the same problems and the problem of criticizing their results are the same. It is the problem of considering the relationships of a finite human being, necessarily circumscribed in his conceptions by his personality, his experience, his ways of thought and the predilections of his period, to something which lies outside all these things and may be called, disregarding for the moment the inconveniences of metaphysical uncertainty, reality.

There are two ways of considering this relationship. One is by considering the observer, and trying to understand what he is trying to do and what is likely to influence him. The other is to turn the other way to try to consider what can be known of what is observed. It is in that direction I wish now to turn. I therefore, with considerable audacity, call my next section 'The Facts'.

6

The Framework of Fact: Interpretations and Legends

Ah! What avails the classic bent
And what the cultured word
Against the undoctored incident
That actually occurred

So WROTE Rudyard Kipling, and for an historian the sentiment is unexceptionable but for two difficulties. It is difficult
to be certain that any account of any incident is undoctored,
and it is often not easy to be quite sure that an incident did
actually occur.

The second doubt need not however be pushed too far.
Putting aside the philosopher's right to doubt everything, there
are many recorded incidents of which one may say with some
certainty that they did occur. There are for instance what may
be called 'the public facts' of history, that is those facts which
are so woven into the texture of human history that, unless
human affairs are an illusion and all history is false, they are
not false.

In the forefront are those incidents on which history turns.
If they had not taken place when they did and as they did then
the rest of history makes nonsense. More than this there are
innumerable contemporary allusions to them, innumerable
allusions in retrospect and, if more were wanted, there are
often descriptions of them by bystanders or participants. For
instance there can be no doubt that the battle of Waterloo was
fought on Sunday, 18 June 1815, and there can be no doubt
who won the battle. If the common opinion on either point was
wrong then most of the history of Europe in the 19th century

would be inexplicable, and a great many contemporary records which allude to the battle, describe the battle, or are concerned with the results of the battle would have to be rejected as spurious. There are also a good many personal accounts left by people who were actually present, so that it is in fact possible to know where most of the important units and personalities engaged were, and what was happening in most parts of the field, at each hour of that terrible Sunday.

The battle of Waterloo is an unusually notable event, but on any reckoning there are a great number of other events which share the same element of certainty. Behind the dramatic turning points of history there are a very large number of more prosaic facts which are not really open to question, the meetings of Parliaments, the passing of laws, the decisions of law courts, much of the routine work of public offices. There are also what might be called incidents of common notoriety, such as the activities of well-known personalities or crimes and disasters that excite public interest. In the background are the private activities of innumerable people, activities which are controlled by, or at least refer to, public events but which have left their own records. Behind these again are the buildings and physical objects which human beings have left behind them. Each of these separate forms of evidence supports the facts established by the others so that the whole fits together as one effective morticed *framework of fact* on which history can rest.

It is only the framework on which history can rest, it is not history. History to mean anything must be more than a rehearsal of facts, it must include an interpretation of the facts.

For instance motives must be supplied to the actors, for observed facts will not by themselves establish the motives of any man or woman. When the circumstances of a man's life are known with some particularity, when many of his letters are available, when his private conversations have been carefully recorded, when perhaps his private reflections have survived in a diary, there still remains a gap in our knowledge of his personality which has to be filled by hypothesis and supposition. But when, as is normally the case, much less has survived, the historian must add much more to recreate a character. It is not, however, only the recreation of human characters that is necessary. Even to forge a coherent story out of the disconnected pieces of separately recorded information may require critical and imaginative powers of a high order. When that is done there will probably be the difficult task of attributing causes and tracing results, and then, if the meaning of the event is to be sought, an attempt must be made to delineate the possible pattern of a whole period or phase of history.

To turn back to the battle of Waterloo. To know that a battle was fought at a particular place on a particular day and who won it is something, but clearly the battle carries much more meaning than that. In order to extract its meaning it is probably necessary to know as far as possible what happened during the battle; and, in order to be able to give a reasonably reliable account of what they believe did happen, historians have had to sort out what was true in a good many different reports left behind by excited, bewildered men, who often could not see very far into the murk of battle, and sometimes to speculate to fill in the gaps in the narrative which are not covered by reliable witnesses. They have had also to eliminate a rather unusually large crop of stories which seem to have been supplied by a love of the picturesque or the dramatic, or in many cases by national vanity. Having done all this the historians were, however, only at the beginning of their task. They have had not only to describe what they thought happened, they had to explain it, to explain it not only in terms of chance or circumstance, but also in terms of human intention, or motive, or will, including what is normally almost contemptuously neglected, the motives of the men actually fighting.

For what was it that made so many men expose themselves so recklessly that day to the dangers of mutilation and death? What made Napoleon's soldiers drive so furiously, so recklessly, up the slopes on to Wellington's carefully sited position? What made the English, the Scots—and the Irish—resist so obstinately in that position till evening and the Prussians arrived? The answers to those questions are important to anyone who is interested in the effect of the human will on the course of history, for there were troops under the Duke's command who were not so well prepared to accept those risks, and if more of his army had been of their mind the course of history would have been different.

Equally important is what was going on in the minds of the two commanders, Napoleon and Wellington, each watching the battle anxiously and trying to control it, till the moment that Wellington realized that victory was under his hand and gave the order for his whole line to advance.

And lastly there is the most important question of all. What was the meaning of what happened? What forces were they which grappled in mortal conflict in Belgium that day? What was the result for humanity when Napoleon's army left the field in irredeemable disorder?

And in this case, as in many others, the meaning of what did happen can only be understood if the probable meaning of what did not happen is considered at the same time. To understand the results of an allied victory it is necessary to envisage the probable results of an allied defeat. Such a defeat had been possible. When La Haye Sainte, the fortified farm house in the centre of Wellington's position, had fallen and before the pressure of the Prussians on Napoleon's right had become overwhelming, victory was almost within the grasp of the French. What then would have happened if Napoleon had driven the English off the field and afterwards turned and crushed the Prussians? Could Napoleon have won the war? Could he have imposed his settlement upon Europe instead of the settlement of Vienna? If he had done so would his régime have been a harsh restless military empire as unrepresentative of the peoples of Europe as were the governments of the old régime? Or would Europe have inherited some of the legacy of the French Revolution without the return to reaction after 1815?

Unless these questions, which are in the last resort unanswerable, are asked the problem of the significance of the battle of Waterloo cannot even be defined. But to consider such questions in order to try to estimate what may have been the result of men's actions, as also to guess what is happening in their thoughts, requires qualities of mind which a mere knowledge of the facts can never give. Indeed the imagination and insight which can enlighten these problems could do so even when knowledge of the facts is less complete than it could be or when liberties have been taken with the facts. That is why an old-fashioned history written by a man of insight and genius can be of more value than a modern one written by a pedant and heavy with the results of the most recent research. That is, also, why an historical novelist can sometimes give an insight into the past which many historians, who stick to the fenced pathway of what is probable and accurate, cannot give.

Nevertheless it is very dangerous to neglect or to tamper with any part of the framework of fact. The facts are the only part of history about which there is any degree of certainty; all interpretation, all reconstruction, is speculative, and if it does not respect the facts speculation is certainly worthless and may be deceptive. If there is any value in the work of an historian whose knowledge of the facts is less than our own, or of an historical novelist who takes liberties with the record of the facts, it can only be because what he does not know, or what he alters, is relatively of less value than what he has produced. But it is very difficult to be sure of that. Clearly the omission of relevant facts from an argument, or the citation of what has become demonstrably untrue, can rob an interpretation of history of any significance, and in any particular case it is necessary to think carefully whether this has happened. No sentimental affection for old and tried authorities, no natural distaste for the inconvenience of historians, who are apparently unable to do more than produce a proliferation of articles and monographs, can unfortunately modify this necessity. While an alteration even in the order of events of a story can so affect the significance of what happened that what a novelist, or a playwright, or the producer of a film, gives to the public so far from giving a new insight into history may be a gross perversion of the truth.

It seems clear from the liberties they take with historic events and characters that there are many people, particularly the producers of films on historical subjects, who are not much troubled by this. Yet even if all that was in question was the production of an interesting story it might be suggested that this attitude is a mistake. The departure from history is very often a departure towards the commonplace. The mind relieved from this disconcerting challenge of fact normally reverts to the world of its own prejudices, and what happens there tends to repeat the commonplaces to which a man is used, and to confirm his pre-existing likes and dislikes. It is for this reason that so often in historical films interesting and challenging historical episodes are reduced to conventional clashes between stereotypes. But there is more in question than the interest of the story. Historical novels, plays and films are dealing with the names of people who once lived and with situations, nations and classes that can be identified. Men and women will believe what they report about the dead, and it will affect their view of the living. If what is implied is untrue and if it reflects, as it is likely to do, political or nationalistic prejudice, it may very well add its small contribution to the misunderstandings and hatreds of the world.

For these reasons, though the framework of fact is not history, it is desirable that anyone who is going to trade in history should treat the discipline it offers with respect, and in order to do this it is important to try to differentiate between the facts upon which history rests on the one hand and on the other the interpretations of history, the judgements about historical events and personalities, the reconstruction of history which may indeed shew what history is about. This however may not be easy to do. The framework of reliable fact never covers the whole of life, and how far it goes at any time will be to some extent a matter for individual judgement. The main points, the principal members so to speak of the framework, are not open to reasonable question, but there are a good many facts about which there may be uncertainty and dis-agreement. They may be isolated and uncorroborated, or only based on uncertain evidence, or it may only be possible to deduce their existence by inference from known facts. Judge-ment on these matters ought of course to be separated from the general interpretations of the meaning and pattern of history, it ought to be directed as objectively as possible at the relevant evidence to the exclusion of everything else. But though it is important to work with that ideal in view it is not possible to attain it. You cannot divide up the human mind into com-partments, and what a man thinks has happened must be to some extent determined by what his general view of the meaning and pattern of history tells him was likely to happen.

As far as paucity of knowledge goes these difficulties will obviously increase the further you go back in time. There is a good deal of evidence about what happened in the remote past. Recorded history of one sort or another goes back a long way, there is often a great body of legend which contains within it some memory of historic events and in addition to this there is the knowledge which scholars have been able to extract from linguistic and archaeological evidence. But even so there must be increasingly large gaps in the framework of reliable facts available. The records will become sparser, there will be more human situations and human activities of which no record has survived, and where there is evidence it may lack other forms of evidence to corroborate it and explain it. Without such external assistance each form of evidence exhibits its peculiar limitations. Unless additional evidence is available the work of the greatest of ancient historians remains the personal view of one man, whose authorities cannot be checked and whose critical standards may not be the same as ours. Without written evidence the relation of the discoveries of the philologist and archaeologist to the general course of history must be largely speculative and inferential, and to enter the world of ancient legend is too often to enter a world of mist, where it may be idle to hope for any authentication of the facts suggested, or any certain way to identify the ghostly personalities and shadows of events which stream in from beyond the frontiers of recorded history.

As history comes down towards modern times the framework of fact will become closer knit and more massive. There will be a greater body of corroborated history. More records will survive. The machinery of government, and in due course the oversight of newspapers, will cover much of what is happening several times over. Nevertheless it is important to recognize that a reliable framework of fact has never covered the whole of life. Things have always been done which have left no record at all and lives lived of which, if there is any record, it will only be of their beginning and ending. Even where there is some record the evidence it may present may well be equivocal and uncorroborated. Where the evidence is lacking a man's general sense of the pattern of history, the historical myth which he uses, will fill in the outline, as it will constantly suggest to him how what he does possess must be extrapolated and interpreted; but what he so supplies will be supposition and not knowledge.

Understandably, but unfortunately, ordinary people who are not professionally concerned with history are not aware of much of this. They are not always aware how little of the past can be known with any certainty. They are not often aware of the extent of their own ignorance. So far from discriminating between the facts behind history and interpretations of history or judgements upon actions in history, their memory of the facts is often of the vaguest and they often remember interpretations or judgements as facts. The Reformation was a 'good' or 'bad' thing according to tradition or temperament. The development of British power in India was something to be ashamed of, or proud of, its surrender a pitiful betrayal or a necessary restitution, according to the way in which ignorance and prejudice direct. The Industrial Revolution can be said to be a bad thing without knowing exactly what or when the Industrial Revolution was. With most men and women any number of these perfunctory judgements do duty for the facts of history and inform their opinions on current affairs. If they took account of the facts behind those judgements, the judgements themselves might have to be abandoned and replaced by opinions which have been reached with greater difficulty and as a result are probably less clear-cut and less confident.

It is difficult to suggest the cure for this. Ordinary men and women cannot be expected to discover all the relevant available facts behind the historical problems which concern them. It may indeed not be at all easy for anyone to distil the facts out of the literature on the subject. Nor can an ordinary man or woman be expected to read all the literature on any subject which is important to them. What can perhaps be suggested is that men and women should realize more fully than perhaps they do that without such knowledge a judgement is likely to be ill-informed and misleading, that if a matter is really important for them they would be well advised to read a scholarly book on the subject, or better still two scholarly books on the subject written from different angles, and that they will do well to scrutinize very carefully a good deal that presents itself to them as history, for much of it will be based not on properly established fact but on legend, that is stories for which no authority can be found.

In all ages legends are among the by-products of history. Their origins are various. Sometimes they are simply history which has slipped from its moorings owing to the fact that what might have authenticated it has got lost. Sometimes they are accounts of encounters, events, conversations of which by their nature there could be no record at the time and for which the only possible evidence is the recollection at a later date of someone who was present. Such evidence of course varies greatly from very accurate memories to the flimsiest gossip often not at first hand, but, even at its best, uncorroborated evidence based on the memory of one man is unsatisfactory, and most gossip and rumours should be regarded with great suspicion. Some legends, however, have not got even contemporary gossip behind them, for a good many legends from all periods are no more than the product of the incurable human instinct to adorn tales, point morals, repeat jokes and recount what seems picturesque or marvellous. And some legends are simply lies which have been made up for the purpose of propaganda.

Most old-fashioned history books which were intended for the young were full of legends, and there were a number of legends which became part of the common inheritance of English history as it used to be taught. They have been told repeatedly. They have been portrayed in pictures in any number of styles. They have been used as texts for moralizing and the basis for jokes. They have been misremembered in every detail and their intended point often mistaken or reversed, as seems normally to be the case nowadays with the story of Canute and the waves. Very few people have troubled to ask what relation they bear to historical truth, but the evidence for some of the more famous ones has been investigated by Dr Birley in a pamphlet published by the Historical Association.[1] The results are amusing but rather devastating. Some favourite stories appear for the first time several centuries after they are supposed to have happened, and then on dubious authority. Sometimes these in fact clearly come into existence at a later date and are fictions; but sometimes legends do seem to be the reflection of something which really took place.

[1] Robert Birley, *The Undergrowth of History*, Historical Association, 1955 (General Series G.30).

Probably none of this matters very much. Sometimes stories have been used to make a misleading gloss to history. For instance there seems to be a not quite contemporary tradition that a game of bowls was being played at Plymouth when the news of the advent of the Armada arrived; a later tradition associates Francis Drake with it and more tentatively suggests that he insisted on finishing the rubber. This rather shadowy story had been elaborated into a piece of braggadocio which probably misrepresents the man and the moment. On the other hand the unexpected corroboration of an old story may bring one suddenly into the company of a great man long dead. For instance the story that the idea of gravity was suggested to Sir Isaac Newton by the fall of an apple has often been dismissed as apocryphal. It used to rest solely on the authority of Voltaire, who might have got it from Newton's niece. However independent confirmation has turned up in the memoir of Newton by his friend Stukeley. Stukeley tells how when they were drinking 'thea' in a garden in London in 1726 something reminded Newton of that historic moment in the orchard at Woolsthorpe Manor so many years before, and he told Stukeley the whole story of how the apple fell and the thoughts to which its fall gave rise.[1]

Generally, however, these stories escape into mist and in most cases it would be best not to pursue them very far. They are old friends and it would be indecent to insist upon seeing their credentials. Nor would it serve any useful purpose. They have given pleasure and it would be difficult to say of most of them that they have ever done any harm to anyone.

There are, however, some legends which are not so innocent. Periods of stress and conflict—the century of the reformation, the religious wars of the 17th century, the revolt of the American Colonies, the potato famine in Ireland, the civil war in the United States and its aftermath in the South and so on and so forth—normally leave a heavy crop of legend behind them. It is never easy to generalize about their authenticity. Some are no doubt the reports of things which really happened, some have been palpably invented, many are the distillations of long and angry brooding on unhappy far-off things. Even

[1] W. Stukeley, *Memoirs of Sir Isaac Newton's Life*, ed. H. Hastings White (1936), pp. 19—20.

when the nucleus of a story is based on reality, its details and its significance may be misleading, since the details may well have been distorted by a misunderstanding of the unfamiliar conditions of a historic situation that has passed away and are likely to have been coloured and shaped in such a way that the significance of the story should be clear and one sided.

For those who repeat these stories, and often succeed in projecting them into the history books, are likely to have one thing in common. They are likely to be partisans. The most normal reason for preserving and retailing stories about the past is in order to celebrate the heroism of a particular party or nation and to draw attention to its sufferings, or to expose the cruelty and perfidy of its opponents. The object is in fact to excite admiration, or pity, or anger. These emotions are very potent emotions, and, as has been said, they can be more easily and powerfully excited by a story than by an abstract argument.

As a result those who are committed to one side of an historical conflict are likely only to repeat the legends which favour their side. This partisan eclecticism can go on for a strangely long time. For instance even nowadays Roman Catholic and Protestant historians when writing about the 16th century are apt to concentrate on the heroism of their own martyrs without paying much attention to what was being dared and endured by the other side, or inflicted by their own. There is, however, a stranger phenomenon than that. When a conflict is over historians are too inclined to take the case for one side and all its partisan stories straight into the canon of history without looking at the evidence, or trying to find out what the other side may have had to say. And what is more, this acceptance is often shared by the natural descendants of those against whom the stories are told.

It seems as if the strain and trouble of trying to take a critical view of confident assertions so troubles the human mind that men and women are prepared to concede the most damning case against their fathers and grandfathers in order to avoid the tedious work of disentangling the evidence for themselves. There is often, also, something other than indolence behind this acquiescence. A gratifying sense of magnanimity can be induced by freely accepting old accusations against one's grandparents, a sense that a sacrifice of pride has been made to serve the cause of general good feeling and justice. The feeling is normally spurious. The sacrifice of pride has usually been negligible, and is amply compensated for in many cases by an enjoyable sense of virtue. What has often been sacrificed is truth and that is a sacrifice which cannot normally be afforded in these contexts.

For many of these stories should be known for what they are, emotive legends which have the property of perpetuating hatred and dislike. They may be true, or have their roots in truth; if so they must not be evaded but fairly considered within their historical context together with all the relevant historical facts stated as impartially as possible. But there is clearly no case for allowing the record to remain loaded with stories which are either demonstrably untrue, or at best unsupported, or, as told, misleading and unfair.

The work of disentangling truth from falsehood is wearisome and difficult. Each story has to be treated separately, and as far as possible traced to its source. There is a temptation to try to avoid this trouble by the general rejection of all the stories of a particular group, but this may be as deceptive as the general acceptance of all the stories in that group would have been. For instance during the war of 1914–18 a great many stories of German atrocities in Belgium and Northern France got into currency. It became clear after the war that many of these were either extremely doubtful, or definitely false. Some had been the result of hysterical rumour, such as often develops in the time of war, which is normally a time of high public credulity. Some were given currency for propaganda purposes by people whose critical standards were low, or who were not anxious to exercise them on that material. Some seem to have been deliberately made up. After the war British writers quite rightly exposed these legends, and the view gained general acceptance that all stories about German atrocities in France and Belgium were without foundation. This unfortunately was not true, as could have been realized if the Belgian records had been searched. As a result information was withheld from the peoples of the world which it was important for them to know, not in order to excite hatred against the Germans, but as a factor in human affairs which they ought to take into account.

It is no doubt desirable that the task of clearing the ground should be done by historians drawn from those nations whom the old legends favoured, and on occasion this has been done with an exemplary devotion to truth. For instance, it was historians from the United States who removed from the best American history books some of the highly disputable matter that had developed in connection with the revolt of the American colonies. Perhaps however the most remarkable example of work of this sort has been the reassessment of the Irish potato famine by Irish historians. That famine stretches across Irish history as one of their greatest national calamities, and it provides some of their bitterest accusations against England. Yet in a book of essays edited by scholars from the national university in Dublin[1] a number of Irish historians have succeeded in giving a more balanced and critical account of the famine and of the behaviour of the British government than is available elsewhere, and they too have managed to eradicate some of the most venomous legends that have flourished from this very fertile soil. Nevertheless none of this work should be thought as the peculiar prerogative of the historian of any one nationality. The object is not to reverse any nation's view of its past but to eliminate what is founded on falsehood, and when he is performing that elementary work an historian's nationality, class or religion ought to be irrelevant.

This work is part of the all important task of bringing everything that passes for history into as close relationship as is possible with provable fact. The interpretation of history can never be supplied by the facts alone, but any interpretation which makes use of facts which can be shewn to be false, or accepts as certainly true facts which are dubious, or does not take into account facts which are known, or could be found out, must be deeply suspect as being at best potentially misleading, and possibly grossly, and dangerously, deceptive. Therefore the relationship between what is to pass for history and prov-

[1] *The Great Famine*, edited by Professors R. Dudley Edwards and T. Desmond Williams of University College, Dublin (Dublin 1956).

able, or for that matter probable, fact is extremely important. It is a relationship which in a great many cases must be subject to continual consideration and reconsideration. This is partly because the work of historical research is constantly going on and new facts are constantly being discovered which make old interpretations impossible. Historians are constantly probing and re-interpreting what was reasonably accepted as fact, and both cancelling old beliefs and discovering new and significant facts. They give and they take away, and any historical conception which has not been adjusted to their most recent results will cease to be satisfactory. There is, however, another, and more cogent, reason why it is important this work should go forward. The relationship between much that passes as history, much indeed that plays its part in exciting the passions and hatreds of mankind, and what can be admitted to be acceptable fact has never been critically considered, and to this untested mass more is unavoidably being added every day as human affairs go forward. It is not only a matter of considerable importance that as much of this as is possible should be tested as soon as is possible, but also that anyone who is likely to be affected by it should realize where the evidence for any part of it appears to be defective or unsatisfactory. It is for this reason important that any educated person should learn something of the procedures which men have developed to test the evidence for what claims to be accepted as historical fact.

Those procedures may require the use of certain specialized techniques. There are for instance the techniques of modern archaeology. There is palaeography, the science of ancient ways of writing, and diplomatic, the science of the forms of documents. There is philology, the science of language and bibliography, the science concerned with the making and distribution of printed books. There are the various chemical tests which men use nowadays in testing for forgeries. These techniques are not for the non-expert, though it would be as well for anyone who is interested to realize that they exist and what they can do. However at the centre of all this specialized activity there is a procedure so simple that anyone should be able to use it without difficulty, for it only consists in asking of any statement that is presented to one certain critical questions.

Indeed the primary difficulty that this procedure presents is that of remembering to ask the questions, for the questions themselves are normally simple and their purport is obvious. In fact the master questions are the most obvious of all. They are, as a general question: 'What is your authority for saying this?', and, as a particular question: 'How do you know that this happened in the way that you say it happened?'

They are questions which both historians, and men and women who are not historians, ought to learn to ask much more often than they do.

7

Observation and Inference: Direct and Indirect Evidence

PROBABLY the most satisfactory and conclusive answer to the question: 'How do you know that this happened as you say it happened?' is: 'I observed it'. This normally means: 'I saw it', but there may also be added: 'I heard it', and it may be: 'I smelt it', and perhaps: 'With my own hands I handled the result'. These answers are not absolutely conclusive. Leaving aside the possibility of fraud, the possibilities of mistake are great, particularly when what is in question is a series of events which happened swiftly leaving no unmistakable evidence of their nature behind. A favourite experiment in law schools has been to enact a rather complicated scene before a large class of students, who are then required to write separate accounts of what happened. The results normally amply prove how various can be the memories of men and women who have very recently seen the same thing. Experience also shews that an interval of time introduces fresh divergencies, not only between different witnesses, but between the accounts given by the same witness at different dates.

But the answer to the question: 'How do you know this happened?' is more likely to be not: 'I myself observed it', but: 'I learnt about it from someone else'. That answer must throw the question one stage further back so that it becomes: 'How did your informant know that this happened?'. That may lead back to another informant, indeed to a line of informants, which in the end reach back to the original observer. It is important to follow up that line in order to find out who the original observer was. It may be difficult to find him. If what is being examined occurs in a history book the answer which the historian may in the end have to give is that he copied it from another historian, who in fact copied from another historian, and so on until at last the statement disappears altogether as an unsupported speculation, or evaporates into an unsubstantial cloud of contemporary rumour and legend. If the statement comes from the daily papers the line may go back by much shorter stages to a bold guess based on incomplete, and perhaps very uncertain, information.

There is however another type of answer to the question: 'How do you know that this happened?' It is this: 'I inferred that it happened from the evidence before me'. This is the answer which would account for most of the results of historical research. Chronicles, charters, registers, the private papers of politicians and business men, newspapers and anything else that may be relevant have been scrutinized and compared, and from the evidence a narrative of events has been assembled.

Probably most of the evidence used in this process will be indirect evidence, that is evidence left by men and women who were intent on their own business and had no intention of leaving behind the information which is being used. In many ways it is the most satisfactory kind of evidence. Those who produced it were unaware of the ghostly figure of the historian standing beside them and therefore did not modify their words to impress him, or lie to deceive him. The people with whom they were in communication were contemporaries who knew a great deal more about what was going on at the time than will ever find its place in the fullest record, and this must both have checked and coloured what was written to them. In addition both writers and recipients are quite likely to have been engaged in some transaction in which a mistatement by any of the participants would not only be pointless, but would cause great inconvenience or even possibly a disaster.

Nevertheless the use of inference introduces a new source of uncertainty. Two questions must be asked of any inference: 'Is the reasoning on which the inference is based correct, and is it the only inference which can be reasonably drawn from the facts?' Clearly the degree of certainty with which an inference can be asserted varies a good deal according to the nature of the inference and of the facts used. For instance an archaeologist finds a building which he is sure has been burnt.

Using all the information at his disposal he puts a date to the burning, and since he knows that this date was in a period of barbarian invasions he therefore concludes that barbarian invaders burnt the building. There may be various inferences here producing various degrees of certainty. The inference that the building was burnt may in fact raise no real problem at all. The state of the walls, the scorched stones, the mass of charred wood and the state of the other objects found in the building may leave no doubt, and the inference can perhaps be promoted to the status of *evident fact*. The inference about the date of the burning may on the other hand be a different matter, the steps by which it was established may have been complicated and technical, and other archaeologists may be unable to accept the reason by which it has been supported. If however in due course the archaeologist's argument comes to be generally accepted his inference about the date may be promoted from a doubtful to a *probable deduction*, and if the date of the burning remains within a period of barbarian invasions it may seem to be natural to go forward to the assumption that it was burnt by barbarians. Yet on closer inspection it may become clear that this assumption can never be proved, that there is nothing in the evidence available which makes it impossible that the building was burnt by a domestic enemy or by accident, and that no further argument or research can enlighten the matter. The inference therefore which started as a *likely guess* may never be accepted as something nearer certainty.

The greatest danger for those who use inference is that they should confound the likely guess with the evident fact, and the danger is the greater because the likely guess often slips into a statement so naturally and easily that it is not realized that any inference has been made at all. A good deal that passes for direct observation is, in fact, really inference. Some actions have been directly observed and it is inferred that others which seem to be their logical complement must have taken place. Indeed they fit so naturally, and apparently inevitably, into a common pattern with what has been observed that it is reported that they have been observed too, and after quite a short time the observer may clearly remember seeing and hearing them.

Yet he may well be mistaken. He may not have seen but

inferred what he believes he saw, and, what is more, the
inference which prompted his false memory may also be
mistaken; indeed it may be possible to prove that what he
claims to have seen never actually took place. A good many
conjuring tricks depend for their success upon the audience
mistaking inference for observation. It is a very dangerous
habit and has no doubt been responsible for many mis-
carriages of justice in the law courts. For instance when a crime
has been committed and a figure has been obscurely seen near
the place of the crime at the time at which it probably happened,
it has sometimes been only too easy for observers, not only to
identify the figure with a known suspect, but after a time to
say without intending deceit that they actually saw the man
there, and recognized him.

In saying this they may have been influenced by a trick of
the mind which sometimes affects testimony in a court of law
and can be encouraged by an over masterful prosecuting
counsel or interrogating policeman. It could be called the
challenge of the false dilemma. It could present itself to a
witness in this reflection: 'If it was not the accused person
that I saw who was it? If I cannot give another name to the
person I saw it must have been him'. Put as simply as that it is
obvious that it will not only be normally dangerous as an
argument but very often absurd, for in many cases there is
probably no ascertainable limit to the number of people it
might have been. But it is unlikely to emerge in a man's mind
so simply and consciously as that, and when it is not expressed
clearly it may not seem so obviously absurd. As a result it
becomes more dangerous. Such a dilemma turns up from time
to time in the treatment accorded to the evidence in the law
courts, sometimes openly, more often implicitly. An interesting
example of it is in the famous case of George Henry Wallace
tried in Liverpool in 1931 for murdering his wife. The events
which led up to the murder were strange. The prosecution
claimed that they could produce an explanation of them on
the premise that Wallace was guilty; the defence could not put
forward so cogent an alternative theory. The Judge warned the
Jury that they must ask for positive proof that the prosecution's
explanation was the right one and not let their hands be forced
by the dilemma, 'If not Wallace who?' Nevertheless the Jury

brought in a verdict of guilty and it is impossible on reading the trial not to believe that that dilemma had weighed heavily with them. The Court of Criminal Appeal took the extreme step of quashing the verdict completely on the ground that there was insufficient positive evidence to support a conviction.[1]

It does not require a counsel for the prosecution to put a false dilemma to an observer; an observer can put such a dilemma to himself. He can say: 'If I have observed things aright what I have observed will agree with what I expected', or 'with what I believe to be probable', or 'will have a rational explanation'; and then go on to say: 'If it does not do these things then my observation was wrong and must be amended accordingly'. Obviously this reflection may have very unfortunate results. The danger of thinking that what you have seen must have been what you expected to see need not be emphasized, and the other two tests are not the logical and compulsive tests that they pretend to be. What a man thinks is probable is, as was suggested in an earlier chapter, to some extent personal to himself, and the kind of 'rational explanation' in which a man is prepared to believe is normally in reality an extension of his sense of probability. Clearly it is very unsatisfactory that a man should amend his memory of what he actually heard and saw in order that it should correspond with what he believes it was likely that he should hear and see. It would be far better if an observer could repeat simply and directly what he actually observed with all its imperfections and improbabilities and leave any explanation, or inferences or suggested editing, to be done as a separate action afterwards.

It is however idle to hope that observers will always do this. There is a natural tendency among all human beings to confuse what they have actually heard and seen with what they have inferred, and to edit it and rationalize it in order to make it correspond with what they believe to be probable or possible. The only thing to do is to try to take this tendency into account, and to remember that what men and women believe to be probable will not only be in some ways peculiar

[1] W. F. Wyndham-Brown. *The Trial of W. H. Wallace edited with an introduction by W. F. Wyndham-Brown*, (1933). Maurice Moisewitch. *4 Famous Trials Retold by Maurice Moisewitch with commentaries by Lord Birkett* (1963).

to themselves, but is likely to be very different indeed in different periods of history and in different groups of people at the same period, and that what men and women think they remember, indeed probably what they think that they see and hear, will normally be affected by this factor.

Of course where an element in the evidence is something which has a continuing physical existence the situation may very well be different. In such case whoever has to use the evidence may not have to depend solely upon the impressions, or the memories, of a witness whose testimony may be marred by a variety of human failures one of which is likely to be the failure to differentiate between inference and observation. He will be able to consider something which has an objective existence outside the mind of the witness and to which he may possibly have personal access himself. The human element will still come in. However obvious may be the message of a physical object it can not frame that message itself. It will need a human being to interpret it, and that necessity must introduce into the matter the element of human judgement, and therefore of uncertainty. But the problems involved will not be the same as those raised by evidence which can only depend on someone's ephemeral observation and on memory.

It is important to make this point here, since most historical work is in fact grounded upon continuing existing material. Relatively little history depends solely on human memory, and what does so is by general agreement normally the least reliable historical work. The next series of questions to be considered must therefore be those which concern the interpretation of the material upon which historical work is likely to be based.

8

Documents Genuine and Spurious

EXCEPT FOR a certain amount of archaeological material, the use of which has its own rules, most of the raw material for historical work is to be found in some sort of document. There are an infinite number of different types of document but there are certain routine questions which ought to be asked of all documents. They are obvious questions and in many cases the answer will be so obvious that it will seem to have been silly to have asked them. Nevertheless they may be important and it can do no harm to run over them, particularly since documents as documents, especially formal documents, sometimes have a semi-hypnotic effect on the minds of those who use them and it is important to remember that all documents have been produced by fallible and potentially dishonest human beings, and that before they reach the scholar they may have passed through the hands of others who may also have had their failings, and were also potentially dishonest.

It is well therefore to start with certain primary questions such as: what is the history of the document, how did it come into my hands? What guarantee is there that it is what it pretends to be? Is the document complete? Has it been tampered with or edited? These last questions are peculiarly important when the original is not available and all that can be consulted is a copy or printed version. If the document is genuine there are other questions to be asked such as: in what circumstances and for what purposes was it produced? Who was the author? What was he trying to do? What were his sources of information? What was his bias? How far was he likely to have wanted to tell the truth? For though politicians, business men and divines are unlikely to try to lie to an historian of whom they are unaware, they may very well have had every intention of lying to each other.

To some of these questions I must return, but there is one question which is perhaps not quite so obvious. It is this: 'Am I quite sure that I know what the words used meant to the writer?' Many people tend to assume that words written by other persons were intended to mean what they would have meant, if they themselves had used them. It is often a very doubtful assumption. The force, the implication, even the actual meaning of words can be drastically affected by the identity of whoever it is who is using them, and the circumstances and the date of use. Historically greater or smaller changes in the meanings commonly attributed to words are always going on. A good example of this can be recognized in the change in the meaning of the word *disinterest* in the last twenty years, or as another example there has been an unfortunate change to the trivial and insignificant in the meaning of the word *awful*, which once expressed an important idea; or again in Dr Johnson's dictionary the first definition of the word *enthusiasm* is 'a vain belief in private revelation; a vain confidence of divine power or communication'—a meaning that can be justified by the word's derivation from the Greek. It was in that sense, not in the modern sense of gusto or zeal, that 18th century divines normally used the word, and if that fact had been more continuously realized by 19th century and 20th century writers some rather silly satire on 18th century Churchmanship could have been avoided. In addition to these, often impalpable, changes there are the cases mentioned earlier where historical associations have added a new dimension to words, a dimension which at a later date may disappear as people forget.

Even if the actual meanings of the words used may have remained the same their force and significance may well alter with the alteration of circumstances and the passage of time. For instance there are certain periods which are accustomed to emphatic theatrical language while others are more sober or deal habitually in meiosis. If you take what is said in the more extravagant periods and give it the value it would have in a more sober period you are liable to make serious mistakes about the speaker's state of mind and intentions.

I came across this phenomenon when I was investigating the circumstances which led up to the popular disturbances in Lancashire and parts of Yorkshire in the late summer of 1842. For some time before those disturbances Chartists, and others who one might think would have known better and had not the excuses which Chartists had, had been using language which seemed to portend an immediate appeal to violence. Men (not apparently Chartists) were said to be prepared to take numbers in a lottery to determine who should be the 'executioner' of Sir Robert Peel, the Prime Minister. In October 1841 a young Liberal, not a Chartist, begged to remind Queen Victoria 'that the heads of better Sovereigns had rolled in the dust' and talked of the flag of revolution being hoisted and of the streets 'running with blood', and a good many others had made their contribution in equally exciting terms.

With all this the relatively peaceful outcome and uncertain intentions of 1842 seem inconsistent, and if this contrast had had to be judged by the standards of other periods what happened, or rather what did not happen, would have been incomprehensible, or at least would have taken a good deal of explaining. However, after studying the matter as far as I could I decided that the explanation was relatively simple. This inflated language was natural to large sections of the community at that date, they inhaled it from the plays they saw, the novels and the poems they read and the speeches and sermons they listened to with avidity. Therefore these phrases did not have the same value in terms of human intention that they would have had in other periods.[1]

This is only one instance of the way in which the force and weight of words can differ from one period to another. But it is not only historical differences that have to be considered. A knowledge of the author and the occasion is necessary if the significance of any remark is to be accurately calculated. Moreover, a social class, a religious or economic group, a profession, each of these may attach particular meanings to certain words which will not be the same as those attached by

[1] See G. Kitson Clark, 'Hunger and Politics in 1842', *The Journal of Modern History* (Chicago), Vol. XXV, No. 4, Dec. 1953, and G. Kitson Clark, 'The Romantic Element—1830 to 1850', *Studies in Social History*, ed. J. H. Plumb (1955) VII, pp. 211–239.

other groups in the same period. It is worthwhile considering how different will be the meanings attributed to the words 'gentlemen', or 'Christian', or 'reasonable'—as applied to actions, arguments or prices—by the people of different groups living at the same time. In fact in dealing with each group it is necessary to create an appropriate frame of reference in order to understand what they are saying. Sometimes indeed even an individual will develop his own wholly idiosyncratic use of words which is different from that of anyone else; indeed most people have, to a greater or less extent, their own private use of symbols and special associations. For this reason it is normally a mistake to read one letter from a correspondence without reading others from the same source. In fact really to understand what men are trying to say it is probably necessary to read as widely as possible in the letters and diaries of that group and period. 'Read till you can hear them talking' may be a counsel of perfection, but it is good advice if the words used are really to be understood.

It is not however always enough to know the meaning of a word in common speech. If the documents from which they come have been produced in the course of some specialized routine, such as a commercial transaction which is governed by the custom of a market or legal proceedings governed by the rules and precedents of a law court, words or phrases may have a specialized meaning which will be misunderstood by anyone who does not know the technicalities involved. For instance the words 'vi et armis' in a writ of trespass before 1545 might suggest to an unknowing person that violence had been used, whereas in fact the words were always inserted in such writs and may mean nothing at all. Nor are such things as the harsh technicalities of ancient law the only forms of specialized language that a researcher may have to know; there are subtler forms of routine phraseology. It is said that it is impossible to understand what is really happening, or likely to happen, in a modern government office unless you know the implications of the carefully modulated phrases used in official correspondence, minutes and dockets.

However to understand the meaning of a document which formed part of a technical process it is not only necessary to understand the specialized language in it, it is also necessary to understand the function it was supposed to perform. Not only the phrases used but the information given in it will be all calculated to serve a particular object and can only be understood if both the nature of that object is understood and also the procedure by which it is intended to bring it about. The object to be served may be one which is of no particular interest to historians and the document may be of importance because it carries information which has little to do with its original purpose. There will be some advantage in this if there is the possibility of fraud, for it will not be the information that the historian wants that will have been falsified. But it will have to be realized that the information which the historian wants may be given in a form most inconvenient to him, or, if it is irrelevant to the purpose of the document, it may not be given at all.

It is not only in official documents that the purpose of the documents determines its content and the meaning of the words in it. For instance the early English law reports were made by lawyers for lawyers to draw attention to important points of law which emerged from a case. They are not intended to record anything else, not even necessarily the results of the case. The consideration also applies to a good many private letters; their meaning cannot be understood unless their object is understood, and to understand this it is necessary to know what were the relations of the writer to the recipient, the kind of impression the writer wishes his letter to make and what results he hopes it will have.

The need to consider the objects of writing even extends to the use of a type of document which might be thought to be least likely to have an ulterior object, a private diary. Naturally the ordinary questions must be asked of a diarist: 'Who was he? What were his sympathies and antipathies likely to be? What were his means of knowledge?', and to these should be added another routine question which might have been thought not to be relevant in such a case: 'Why did he write?' It may have been no more than an almost mechanical habit which once developed could not be given up. He may have been inspired by the sheer delight in finding things out and putting them down. He may have written primarily to relieve his feelings, to say things which he could not say in the maddening relationships of ordinary life, or to encourage himself, when he was not certain of himself or others were not certain of him. Or he may have in his mind a shadowy audience before which he wishes to justify himself, or perhaps to prove how great a sinner he has been.

All these different objects will affect what is recorded and the way it is recorded. They are not exclusive of each other, and different motives may affect a man's diary at different times of his life. What militates most against the value of a diary as evidence is the idea, however nebulous, of ultimate publication. It can often be detected in the odd unguarded phrase, and the stronger and more definite it becomes the quicker the diary is likely to sink in the scale of reliable evidence towards the place occupied by the least convincing of all personal records, the memoirs and autobiographies written by eminent persons—particularly by soldiers, statesmen and men and women who have been prominent on the stage—in order to justify themselves.

The only advantage that a diary written for publication may have over these self-justificatory memoirs may be that it may have been written soon after the events recorded have happened, before memory had begun to play tricks, and before the results of what was being done had fully declared themselves. And even that advantage can be forfeited, for diarists have been known to insert passages into the blank spaces of an earlier record, passages written long after the event to prove the foresight of the diarist.

Indeed whole diaries have been forged. The success of Daniel Defoe's performances in that line, his *Memoirs of a Cavalier* and his *Journal of the Plague Year* are worth remembering, and anyone who is interested in the methods which he employed in producing those works would do well to extend their studies to his *Apparition of one Mrs Veal* and to *The Life and strange surprizing Adventures of Robinson Crusoe, of York, Mariner*.

Defoe's technique is carefully discussed by Sir Leslie Stephen in a well known essay.[1] It is a technique which is worth the attention of anyone who is interested in the evaluation of the evidence in what claim to be diaries and memoirs, and in other reports that claim to be the authentic testimony of a

[1] Leslie Stephen, *Hours in a Library*, 3 Vols. (1917). Vol. I, pp. 1–43.

bystander. For though it is possible that Defoe may have used some authentic materials for some of his works, it is quite certain that he was extremely successful in making what was certainly fictitious seem to be authentic. He often starts work with an elaborate discussion of his authorities, rejecting some as unsatisfactory and accepting others cautiously after weighing the evidence, thus disguising the fact that the only evidence that any of them exist at all is his own assertion that they do. As Stephen points out there is a good example of this preliminary exercise at the beginning of *Mrs Veal*. Defoe then goes on to his story which he furnishes with much apparently irrelevant, but probable, detail and tells in a very matter of fact style.

A typical example of his use of detail is the loving account of the various objects Robinson Crusoe was able to get from the wrecked hulk of his ship, and his difficulties in getting them ashore on to his island, having to transport them by a number of extemporized rafts in a series of voyages. Each of his visits to the ship is carefully described down to the moment when he 'rummaged' in the cabin for the last time and found a locker with drawers that would open. In one of these he finds two or three razors, one pair of large scissors and ten or a dozen of good knives and forks, and in another some thirty-six pounds value in money, some European, some Brazilian. The money he apostrophizes. ' "O drug" said I aloud, "What art thou good for? Thou art not worth to me, no, not the taking off of the ground; one of those knives is worth all this heap. I have no manner of use for thee; ever remain where thou art and go to the bottom as a creature whose life is not worth saving". However upon second thoughts, I took it away; and wrapping all this in a piece of canvas, I began to think of making another raft.'

The money is perhaps clearly put in for satiric purposes, but all the rest of the detail of the things he got from the ship, the three dutch cheeses and five pieces of dried goat's flesh, the two saws, the axe and hammer, the two or three bags of nails, the great screw jack, together with the problems that he faced in ferrying his loot ashore and the fact that on one occasion he carelessly allowed some of his clothes to be washed away by the tide and that on another occasion he attached a raft to two broken oars driven into the ground one at the side and one at the end, all seems to be pointless unless these were the things which Robinson Crusoe actually found and did. The whole account seems in fact to be the work of a rather prosaic minded man trying to say exactly what happened as it happened. The details are interesting as practical details in a romantic situation are interesting, but they are not significant, and because of this the description has, still, after nearly three centuries, the ring of truth. Nevertheless Crusoe, wreck and island, are all in reality figments of Defoe's imagination, for he got very little from the true story of Alexander Selkirk, which was his starting point.

Defoe's achievements suggest another problem which has to be considered by all who use documents, the problem whether a document is all that it has been thought to be, whether its authority has been exaggerated or its nature mistaken, or whether there has been fraud.

Fraud in handling documents is likely to take one of three forms. Documents which did not exist may have been created by forgery, existing documents may have been altered, or documents may have been abstracted and destroyed. Of all these expedients the last is probably the most difficult to detect, especially if no one has known the document was there, and it must be remembered that the disappearance of a document may alter the meaning of those which are left as much as the intrusion of one that is spurious.

The tests for forgery are likely to be extremely technical. It is likely that if an actual document is available the writing will have to be examined with the help of a microscope letter by letter and the material on which it is written minutely inspected. An X-ray examination may be necessary. Any ink, or paper, or paste that may have been used may have to be analysed chemically. How technical all this can be may be studied in the book which exposed some of the pamphlets which had been produced by Thomas Wise.[1] Where the

[1] J. Carter and G. Pollard, *An inquiry into the nature of certain nineteenth century pamphlets* (London, 1934). It is worth while to consider the points which it was thought necessary to cover in order to pass off the forgery of some spurious lines by Chaucer in a story by Rudyard Kipling called

original is not available the investigator may have to fall back on internal evidence, on the question whether the facts quoted in the document are consistent with the known facts of the period, or on the style and the nature of the language employed. It will be necessary to ask whether the language of the document is philologically possible for the date to which the document is ascribed. If other better authenticated documents of the same author exist it may be possible to enquire whether the suspect document uses the same style, or whether a word count shews that it uses words with the same frequencies. On a formal document the science of diplomatic can be used. It can be tested to see whether the document uses the formulae and the general arrangement which would be natural or possible in a similar document of the period to which it is ascribed.

All this is of course very skilled work. It requires access to such documents as exist, considerable leisure to study them, the command of the necessary techniques and possibly nowadays the use of a laboratory. These things cannot be available to the ordinary student, who must largely depend on what the specialists will do for him. There are, however, some things he can do to protect himself. He can always look out for facts in the document which are inconsistent with the ordinary framework of fact; the failure to check obvious facts which could be known from other sources is perhaps the human failure which above all others makes fraud possible and easy. If his suspicions are aroused he should always ask about the history of a document. 'Is it known where it comes from, and how it reached its present place of repository? Does it come from some large well-known collection where it was naturally stored immediately after receipt, as for instance the muniment room of a well-known statesman? Or has it emerged from nowhere, perhaps been sold by a dealer or found its way into a collection with which it has no obvious connection?' There is some safety in using documents from a well-established relatively modern collection. It is exceedingly unlikely that spurious material will have been mixed with the genuine document in such collections, and where there has been no

---

'Dayspring Mishandled' (Rudyard Kipling, *Limits and Renewals*, 1932). The forgery is of course fictitious, but Kipling had obviously studied the subject very carefully.

motive for forgery and the collection has a satisfactory history no doubt the documents from large collections of medieval records are reasonably reliable. There is much protection to be gained from the fact that there are very many documents which no one would think it worthwhile to forge, and there is some safety to be gained from the bulk of the work the forger would need to do. A forgery whose success must depend on the faking of a large number of documents, or a very long document, is less likely to have been perpetrated than one which would only need the faking of a single document or a short one. It would be a great mistake, however, to underestimate the possible industry and enterprise of forgers, some of their efforts have been very massive indeed.[1] But it is easier, and safer, to forge a single document than a number of documents, and a short one than a longer one. Perhaps the most suspect documents of all are single documents from important people on important occasions which have no satisfactory genealogy. These are sometimes bought by the unwary; indeed the documents which simple-minded people can be induced to buy are sometimes not forgeries but facsimiles detached from some book. In fact when the surface of the paper on which some of these documents purport to be written is examined it can be seen that they are actually lithographs.

However even if documents come from a large collection of unimpeachable heredity they may still have been tampered with, often by respectable people for what appeared to them to be innocent reasons. A widow or daughter has tried to black out names or sentences, cut pages out of letters or diaries or destroyed letters in order to conceal old animosities, or has excised violent expressions of opinion or expressions which seemed to them to be indecent. Autograph hunters may have cut out pages out of letters, abstracted letters and sometimes by these means wrecked whole collections. Sometimes officious people have put dates at the head of undated letters, which have then been taken as having been placed there by the original writers, but which are in fact wrong.

[1] One of the most massive forgeries in existence must be the famous 9th century forgery of Papal documents, the Psuedo-Isidore Decretals, which in the most recent edition fills 769 pages of small print. (I owe this information to Dr. W. Ullmann.)

The possibilities of fraud are perhaps most serious when historians are working with what may be called official documents, documents with the imprimatur of some public authority. These are peculiarly serious for two reasons, first because official records are apt to form important members of the framework of fact, and secondly because if all documents tend to have an hypnotic effect on the minds of those who use them, the effect of documents which apparently have the endorsement of a public authority is sometimes almost irresistible.

The probability that official documents may have been forged or tampered with increases the further you go back into the middle ages. This is partly because before critical standards were established a forgery was more likely to be successful; indeed there seems to have been a certain amount of what may be called innocent forgery, as when a monastery conceived itself to have received certain rights from a dead king, but could not find the actual document conferring the grant among its muniments, and therefore supplied the loss. But tampering and forgery was also possible because down to comparatively recent times public records and archives were not always kept with the same meticulous care as they are today, nor were they stored in such a way as to prevent subsequent interference with them, or natural loss. Consequently medieval documents may have on occasions notoriously been tampered with, as for instance the Parliament rolls describing the deposition of Richard II have been mishandled; or additions, possibly quite innocent additions, have been made to documents like the famous addition by a later scribe of the title 'Pro Camera Stellata' to a statute of 1487, 3 Henry VII cap. 1, which caused great trouble among the historians of Star Chamber till what had happened was recognized. At times a document has been fundamentally altered by miscopying. For instance an important development in law, the power of justices of the peace to bind unsatisfactory people over to keep the peace, seems to have been derived from the miscopying of a 14th century statute by a 15th century clerk.[1]

---

[1] For the addition to 3 Henry VII cap. 1, see A. F. Pollard. English Historical Review, Vol 37 (1922), pp. 520–4. For the power to bind over, see C. G. Crump and C. Johnson, English Historical Review, Vol. 27 (1912), pp. 226–38.

Some documents have perished. Often enough this has resulted from the ordinary chances which naturally affect a body of documents through several centuries of slovenly custody in poor conditions. They have been stained by damp, eaten by mice, become the last resting place of rats, used as waste paper or simply and casually lost. At times it seems clear that the losses have not been so casual. For instance the disappearance, to which I will return later, of every document written by Judge Jeffreys, or to Judge Jeffreys, from the State Papers for the reign of James II is unlikely to have been accidental. Where the document has not been in the custody of the central offices of State, but in more provincial and casual custody the chances of their being lost, damaged or possibly tampered with have been greater. Perhaps the least secure have been Parish registers. This is a fact which was fully recognized by Victorian novelists who realized the romantic possibilities which a faked entry in a Parish register might offer in a novel which turned on a problem of succession. In this case, indeed, the expedients of fiction were reflected in real life in the series of forged entries which the fifth Earl of Berkeley inserted into the Berkeley Parish register to antedate to 1785 his marriage to Mary Cole which only took place in 1796 and to legitimize his first four children by her.[1]

During the 19th century records in most civilized countries came to be more carefully stored, and the chances of altering them or abstracting them or even of losing them has proportionately decreased. Even so the chances of carelessness varying into minor, and only partially realized, dishonesty, or for that matter the chances of downright fraud can never be wholly eliminated. The operations of Major Henry during the Dreyfus case shew what was possible in France in 1896, and the argument that what can take place in Europe is absolutely prevented by some law of nature from happening on this side of the channel is not a convincing one.

There has certainly been one notable case in Britain in this

---

[1] For the forgeries by the 5th Earl of Berkeley, see *The Complete Peerage*, edited by G. E. C., revised by the Hon. Vicary Gibbs, Vol. II (1912), p. 142 note (d) and p. 143 note (e). I owe this reference to Professor C. R. Cheney. For this and other fraudulent entries in Parish Registers, see *Notes and Queries*, Vol. 155 (July-Dec., 1928), pp. 296, 352–4, 376, 463.

century of an inconvenient document being destroyed. In 1918 Lloyd George as Prime Minister was publicly accused by Sir Frederick Maurice, the Director of Military Operations, of having misrepresented to the country the number of British troops in France at the critical moment of the last German offensive. In debate in the House of Commons Lloyd George declared that he had only given the figures which he had received from Maurice. This was superficially true since the first figures given mistakenly included troops in Italy and it was this inflated figure Lloyd George gave. However the mistake had been recognized at once and a correction immediately sent. It is possible that the Prime Minister never saw, or never took in, this correction, but the document containing it, most inconveniently, turned up a few days after the debate in a box which had been circulated to him. When Lloyd George's private secretary found it he immediately threw it into the fire intending to say nothing about it. If it had not been for the presence in the room at that moment of the lady who subsequently became the Countess Lloyd George, in all probability no one would ever have known what happened.[1]

In fact human nature being what it is there can never be absolute certainty what might happen if an interested official or ex-minister should have a chance of modifying an inopportune document, which as the saying goes 'is open to misconstruction'. But of course in any ordinary modern state there is a large mass of records composed as a matter of routine by disinterested, or uninterested, officials and stored systematically with which it would be difficult to tamper and from which it would not be easy to abstract documents. Indeed the mass is in itself a danger to research, for in order to make ultimate storage a possibility governments have sometimes adopted a policy of rather extensive destruction of documents that officials have held to be of no historic interest. This unfortunately has meant at times that matter which would have been of considerable value to students has disappeared. It could be wished that the British Government would put more of its records on microfilm which would mean that more could

[1] Lord Beaverbrook, *Men and Power* (London, 1956), pp. 258—64. The story is based on an entry in the diary of Frances, Countess Lloyd George of Dwyfor.

be destroyed while at the same time more could be preserved.

However another difficulty confronts anyone who intends to use recent official records. No state can allow completely free access to its most recent records. This does not in any way necessarily mean that it has ugly secrets to hide. There may well be matters in the record, as for instance the expression of uninhibited views by ministers or diplomatists which might complicate relationships with other powers, or even with particular individuals with whom it was still necessary to have dealings. It is also widely held that officials are not likely to express their views frankly if they know that what they have written will be revealed to all and sundry within a reasonably short period, probably in their own lifetime. These are perfectly defensible reasons for withholding documents, but unfortunately they are apt to be vitiated by the way the matter works out. For different countries have different rules in this matter and some permit access to documents and publication much earlier than others do; moreover in many countries, certainly in Britain, exceptions are made so that some people are allowed to use documents the use of which is denied to others. The results are wholly unfortunate. The account of an important transaction may be generally known only in the terms of the official correspondence of a country which has liberated its records. If this is so it stands to reason that the account will be a one-sided one, and something which will do greater harm both to the interest of the government which has withheld its documents, and to international relations, than any revelations could do. So far from civil servants being protected the situation will also be peculiarly hard on the wretched officials of the withholding country, for their actions will be attacked but they will not be permitted to refer to the documents which might enable them to reply. This hardship will, however, be greatly increased if exceptions are permitted by the country which is withholding documents so that favoured statesmen writing their memoirs, and foreigners or journalists whom it is desired to propitiate, are allowed access to documents which is denied to old servants of the government who wish to defend their actions, or historians who wish, if they can, to produce a balanced account of what happened.

For this reason it is necessary to be careful when dealing with recent history which purports to be based on official documents. It may well be that essential information has been withheld, or not discovered, because it is in the archives of a power which has refused to allow to historians the right of unimpeded search. Nor can it be assumed that the information would be to the disadvantage of the withholding power. It is also necessary to use caution in the use of documents which have been published by governments in order to give their own official account of what happened. In a totalitarian state like Russia history has to be changed to synchronize with the change in régime, and the documents are normally changed to agree with the official view of history at that moment prevailing. But even in Britain when documents have been laid before Parliament they have often been edited before they appeared.

Nevertheless with all these reservations documents in official archives are necessarily one of the main, and normally one of the most reliable, sources of information for the historian. Where they refer to the routine business of government they would probably be in most cases not worth mishandling, and if they were tampered with or faked the fact would likely to become clear to others engaged in the same routine. More than this a document with the authority of government behind it does have a guarantee of reliability to back it which a privately produced document is not likely to have. Those who produce it are more seriously responsible for it, and it may have results which may not be misrepresented. This however raises the question: 'What documents can be said to have the authority of the government behind them, and to what extent in any particular case does this give a guarantee of accuracy?' For instance the official record of a trial may be no more than a record of the charge and the sentence, but there may have also survived what appears to be a verbatim report of the trial, and possibly of a speech from the scaffold. Sometimes the report has received some sort of imprimatur from the judge; sometimes indeed the reports of the trial and of the execution were due to government initiative. But these facts do not convert them into official reports; moreover it must be remembered that trials were often of great political interest so that these reports often have a strong propaganda intention. Sometimes indeed they seem to be propaganda not for the government but for the other side. In either case it is at least partly as propaganda not as the account of an official act that they must be judged.

To this I must return. There is, however, another peculiarly cogent example of an unofficial record gaining something like official authority from association with official proceedings. Till 1909 there was in Britain no official report on what was said in Parliament, though there was an official report on what was done. It is often thought that Hansard's Parliamentary Debates were official, but this is not so. They were throughout the 19th century a private venture. At the very beginning of the 19th century William Cobbett—Cobbett of the *Rural Rides* —conceived the idea of a Parliamentary History. Before 1803 it was to be composed from such materials as existed, some of them of very doubtful validity; after 1803 it was to be a synthesis of the reports of Parliamentary Debates which were beginning to appear in the various newspapers, balancing one report against another. Cobbett started on this project but in 1810 he got into trouble for the publication of what was held to be a libel, and consequently went to prison, and was sold up. His property in the reports was sold to T. C. Hansard the printer of the Journal and the reports of the committees of the House of Commons, who carried on the venture.

Hansard's reports of Parliamentary Debates therefore started in 1812 and continued for most of the 19th century. They were not reports taken down in the gallery of either house, Hansard did not have a reporter in the gallery of the House of Commons till 1878; they were as in Cobbett's day a composite report made by combining and balancing the reports of the debates that appeared in the newspapers. Hansard also was prepared on occasion to accept from members revised copies of their speeches, a practice which does not lead to accurate reporting. Nor is there any guarantee that Hansard or his predecessor reported everything that was said or done in Parliament.

Hansard's report was therefore produced privately and for profit. At first it paid so well that the Mirror of Parliament was started in competition. In due course, however, its profits failed and from 1855 the Treasury had to guarantee a number of sets to keep it going. In the last quarter of the century there was considerable dissatisfaction with the situation and the quality of the reports, and a series of Parliamentary committees considered the matter. They however did not achieve very much and in 1889 T. C. Hansard sold out his interest in the reports to what was really a fraudulent syndicate whose main figure was Horatio Bottomley. This syndicate did not last long, and for a period Hansard passed through several hands, and the reporting was extremely inadequate. This unhappy interlude lasted till 1909 when on the recommendation of another committee the government at last took over the business of supplying an official report of the debates in Parliament.

Before 1909, therefore, Hansard does not possess the authority that might come from an official endorsement or from direct reporting, and there are probably occasions when the newspapers, notably *The Times* which had a large body of reporters, are better authorities for what was said than Hansard. This is particularly so when there is an asterisk in the margin of Hansard to shew that a member has revised his speech, though while he was in charge Hansard tried to prevent them doing more than revise their grammar. Probably none of this is of great historical importance, but it is significant that very many people who have used Hansard have not discovered it, but have assumed that Hansard was always an official report.[1]

Another example of the way in which an official association seems to give an official guarantee which is not justified is the respect with which historians sometimes treat the findings of Royal Commissions or of Select Committees of the Houses of Parliament, a respect which is often extended to the evidence given before them. It seems sometimes to be assumed that because they are set up by Crown or Parliament such committees and commissions have been objective enquiries systematically planned by unbiased persons of great intelligence who were only anxious to find out the truth. They were often

[1] Michael Macdonagh, *The Reporters Gallery* (1913), J. C. Trewin and E. M. King, *Printer to the House* (1952), Strathearn Gordon, *Our Parliament* (1964).

anything but that. Many commissions and committees were carefully organized by those who promoted them to drive home a particular point of view, either to support one side in a controversy or to help the passage of certain preconceived legislation. For this purpose the members were chosen, the evidence carefully selected and the proceedings marshalled so that the desired conclusions could be embodied in a report, which could be in the second and third quarter of the 19th century a most effective instrument for the control of opinion.

The result was, naturally, not always a balanced and comprehensive view of all the relevant evidence. That does not of course mean that both special committees and Royal Commissions did not at times in this period collect evidence of the greatest historical importance, still less that some of the most deserving causes were not supported in this way. In fact one of the committees whose methods were most questionable was one whose objects were the most socially desirable. It is the select committee into the conditions of the labour of factory children which Michael Sadler got appointed in 1831 to support the bill he had promoted in their protection. The evidence Sadler collected was very one-sided; it had been supposed that the other side would have a chance to produce evidence to support their case, but the dissolution of Parliament intervened. Sadler was however anxious to gain support for his bill, so that the report was published with Sadler's evidence in it but without any evidence from the other side.

The result is as might be expected not altogether satisfactory if it is to be considered as an unbiased enquiry into a difficult subject. Yet this report has been called in one book: 'a classical document. It is one of the main sources of our knowledge of the condition of factory life at the time' and in another: 'One of the most valuable collections of evidence on industrial conditions we possess'. It is as well to compare these comments with that by Engels: 'Its report was emphatically partisan composed by strong enemies of the factory system for party ends. . . . Sadler permitted himself to be betrayed by his noble enthusiasms into the most distorted and erroneous statements.' Engels was no friend of the factory system and no enemy of Sadler, and a review of the evidence, and of the way in which it was collected and presented suggests that he **was** right.[1]

The moral of all this is a simple one. No document, and no statement, official or non-official, is beyond question. It is perfectly true that in our well docketed, cross referenced, heavily registered age, when documents appear not in battalions but in armies, and after their period of use should sleep secure in inviolable official sanctuaries, recorded facts may be so well corroborated and so essentially a part of the complicated network of modern life, so difficult to fake and so little worthwhile faking, that many officially recorded facts can take their place, almost unquestioned, in the framework of fact upon which history rests. Even so the possibilities of mistake, loss or fraud should never be completely banished from the mind; and the further research is pressed back into the past the more important it is to keep in mind these possibilities.

At no period and in no context is it therefore irrevelant to ask who had made a particular record, what was his object in making it, how and where has the record been kept, and what official warranty it has; and it is always necessary to remember that the opinions of judges and juries, policemen and government inspectors, members of Parliament and people serving on, or appearing before Parliamentary committees and Royal Commissions, should be subjected to the same critical tests as the opinions of anyone else. They may have the awful authority of the state behind them, but they are mortal men and subject to the temptations and limitations of mortal men. It is therefore always legitimate to ask: 'Who were they? What factors were likely to affect their minds? What were they trying to do?'

There are, therefore, many questions to be asked about any document, and the trouble about many of them is that they can never be answered. They certainly cannot be answered by the ordinary unprofessional reader of history, and in many cases no one, work as hard or as skilfully as he may, can

[1] W. H. Hutt, 'The factory system of the early 19th century,' in *Capitalism and the Historians*, ed. F. A. Hayek (Chicago, 1954), pp. 161 ff. c.f. Miss Lucy Brown's account of the methods of the Selection Committee on Import Duties: Miss L. Brown 'The Board of Trade and the Tariff Problem, 1840–2', *English Historical Review*, Vol. 68 (1953), pp. 394–421 and Miss L. Brown, *The Board of Trade and the Free Trade Movement* (1958), pp. 70–5 and 141 ff.

answer them, for the answer has been lost. Even so it may be well to ask them, for it is often important to remember what questions have not been answered. This should not lead to general disbelief, but perhaps to a more general suspension of implicit belief, and to the general habit which makes a man ask of any assertion made to him: 'What is the nature of the evidence that supports this?'

It should be by now clear that to that question a second should normally be added: 'Through whose hands has this evidence passed?'

9

The Intermediaries

THE QUESTIONS 'through whose hands has this evidence passed and what have they done to it' cannot be confined to those who have had documents in their charge. They must be asked of everyone else who has transmitted the evidence upon which the history which men and women are going to use is based. They should be asked of those who have carried evidence in their minds as a contemporary report or as an oral tradition, of those who reported spoken words, of those who copied original documents and of the editors who published their results, and lastly they must be asked of the historians who produce the finished product for the market. Where it is possible it is desirable to find out something about all these people, but if that is not possible it is necessary to consider what they may have done to what they have received.

This question is most obviously relevant to those who have handed on an ancient oral tradition. Nowadays scholars are less cavalier than they used to be in their treatment of oral traditions. They are more likely to believe that they may have started from something that may have really happened to some personality however shadowy and remote, and not from those solar myths or explanatory fables once so beloved by academics. Even so any tradition is likely to have suffered drastic changes in its passage through the centuries. Critical details may have been lost, or added. A story may have been changed to suit the probabilities of a generation other than that in which whatever happened did happen. It may have been taken from the forgotten person who was its original hero and told of some whom everyone remembers like King Arthur, Oliver Cromwell or Winston Churchill. It may have grown so gigantically that it is impossible to identify in it the grain of truth from which it originally sprang.

But it is not only the wear and tear of centuries that makes drastic changes in what is transmitted from mouth to mouth; they can also take place in what passes through a country in a matter of weeks. There was an example of this in the late summer of 1940 when Great Britain was nerving itself to meet a probable Nazi invasion. Towards the end of August a rumour spread through the country that an invasion had indeed taken place and had been repulsed with heavy loss. It was possible to meet people who seemed to say that they had actually seen the German corpses in their myriads on the beaches, while others had seen the German parachutists coming down from the clouds. It was all untrue. The German parachutists had been conjured out of thin air. There were those who when questioned still declared that they had seen them, but it could be proved that in their locality nothing had come down. The German bodies on the shores had more foundation in fact. In August the bodies of about forty dead German soldiers who had probably been caught by British bombers when practising embarkations, were washed ashore between the Isle of Wight and Cornwall. It was from these exiguous beginnings that the whole story had developed.[1]

The incident not only demonstrates how quickly a story can be developed and embroidered, particularly at a time of stress and expectation; but it is also an example of something which happens very often to endorse rumours. It may be called *unreal corroboration*. The rumour of 1940 seemed to be convincing at the time because it was repeated by a good many people who had apparently no connection of any sort with each other. In fact it was almost certainly the same rumour which had started originally from the same group of people, but had travelled rapidly by various routes to converge again on the same recipient, so that the repetitions had no corroborative value at all. What is remarkable in retrospect is the extraordinary confidence with which a great variety of people asserted that what they repeated was based on personal

[1] See Winston Churchill, *The Second World War*, Vol. II (1949), pp. 275–6. I also partly base what I say here about this on personal memories of that time.

knowledge, though always on personal knowledge at second hand.

The untrustworthiness of rumour is, of course, notorious, though it is remarkable how much that springs from that source manages to seep into what is accepted as history. What requires more attention than it usually receives is what may have happened to evidence which is transmitted in seemingly much more reliable fashions, particularly in a printed record. Yet this problem may be all important for the ordinary consumer of history. For the ordinary consumer of history—that is the general reader, the student who is not engaged in historical research or the man or woman who wishes to be informed of the background of a particular transaction or situation—is unlikely to come into contact with any of his evidence at first hand. If he refers to documents they are likely to have been transcribed, edited and published by people who will have come between him and the originals. If he is interested in what has been spoken, a reporter and an editor and a printer have probably intervened, and in many cases some historian will have handled the evidence and served it to him in pre-digested form. It is important therefore for any user of history to consider from time to time what any of these people may have done to the evidence as it passed through their hands. But it is rare for ordinary men and women to do this, particularly when the evidence appears to them to be presented in the exact words which were written and spoken in the past.

Perhaps the most serious difficulties are presented by reported speech. What is represented as direct speech often has a vividness and an immediacy which creates a strong feeling that one is in the presence of the past re-enacting itself without the interference of any human agency. In fact the recording of speech probably presents more problems than any other form of evidence. These problems can be roughly distributed in two groups. First there are the problems connected with the actual taking of the record. 'Who was the reporter? Was he competent and honest? What was his method?

Did he take it down at the time, or memorize it and record it afterwards? If at the time how many words was he able to take down a minute? How much of his own did he have to add to turn his notes into a reasonably coherent account? To what extent did he wish to slant the report and in what direction?' The second group are problems common to all records. They are 'What has happened to the report after it has been made? Has it been mutilated by anyone? To what extent has it been edited for publication?'

In modern times the invention of the tape recording apparatus has supplied what could be completely satisfactory answers to the questions of the first group, but it has made it all the more important to ask the questions in the second group. In an American experiment it was found to be possible so to alter a tape in which the speaker had spoken 'in favour of God, for motherhood and against communism' that after two hours the speaker heard his own voice announcing that, to quote him, 'I had stolen money from the Commonwealth of Pennsylvania, advocated the overthrow of the Government by force and violence and confessed to killing an F.B.I. agent—without additional words added to the tape, without doing anything other than cutting it up and putting it together again'.[1] Very careful tests could not detect any difference between the edited and the unedited tape. This transmutation may have been something of a tour de force, but clearly a much smaller change could make a tape extremely dangerous to the man of whom the record was taken.

Setting the tape recorder on one side there are various ways in which what a man has said can be recorded. To start with the most primitive, it can be memorized. Modern educated people have so damaged their memories by disuse and reliance on the written word that as far as they are concerned memory would be an impossibly uncertain way of recording anything, but in ages when the written word was not generally used or with social groups who do not turn readily to writing, the power to memorize seems to have been much greater. This is

[1] Alan Barth, *The Price of Liberty* (New York, 1961), p. 142, quoting from the Senate Documents of the 85th and 86th Congress. Sub-Committees on Constitutional Rights. Hearings on Wire tapping and the Bill of Rights, Part 3, p. 509.

also true even nowadays of people who have trained their memories. The power to memorize therefore is an important factor to take into account not only when considering the validity of tradition, but when considering the recording of the spoken word before the invention of shorthand. It remains however an uncertain factor. It is certainly not satisfactory to rely for the transmission of a record on one man's memory alone. Such a record would seem to present disadvantages of any record made by a single-handed reporter but in an exaggerated form. There can be no exterior check. The memorizer may not have heard aright. He may have misunderstood what he heard and replaced it by something he did understand which it resembled. He may not have thought that the actual words mattered and supplied words of his own, still in direct speech. If he did not record what he heard fairly soon after he had heard it he may have changed it in his mind in ways that no one can recover. Moreover experience shews that a claim, at least by a modern writer, to repeat from memory conversations in direct speech is normally a danger sign, and that more often than not both the conversations and the account that contains them are questionable, or at best hazy and inaccurate.

If people speak slowly it is possible to take down what they say in long hand. In this way interrogations seem to have been taken down. This can be done with such accuracy that in the records of the interrogations in 16th century Catalonia of prisoners under torture every oath and expression of pain was apparently noted. What is spoken at greater speed can be, after some sort, recorded if men use abbreviations, such as were widely used in the Middle Ages. These were no doubt used in the reporting of the cases in the law courts in medieval England. There is, however, a limit to what can be done by the use of abbreviations. Conventional symbols can be provided for frequently used words like conjunctions and prepositions, for the common endings of words like genitive plurals in Latin, and for phrases and proper names in habitual use in the particular business which is being reported, if that business is sufficiently specialized. On the other hand it is impossible to charge the memory with enough symbols and abbreviations to cover every possible word or phrase that might turn up in more general discussions. Therefore, though the systems of abbreviations were no doubt very effective in assisting the recording of more or less specialized business, such as the technical side of the business of a law court, where the same words and phrases constantly recurred, they would be of much less use in giving a continuous record of a general discussion which might constantly introduce words and phrases for which there was no symbol. To record such a discussion satisfactorily a general system of shorthand is probably necessary based on alphabetic, syllabic or, best of all, phonetic principles.

A system of shorthand was known in the ancient world. It was called after its inventor the Tironian system and the knowledge of it remained in Italy well into the Middle Ages, but the first real system of shorthand in England was that published by a clergyman called Timothy Bright in 1588. This, however, was so clumsy as not to be of general use and it is not till the 17th century that more practicable systems began to appear.

There was already a demand for it. The use of the printing press had made possible the wide diffusion of accounts of contemporary events. Among those events which excited the widest interest were important trials, which, as has been said, also had considerable propaganda value, as the Tudor government realized when for instance they placed Thomas Norton the Queen's printer in an advantageous position at the trial of the Duke of Norfolk in 1572 in order that he might write an account of it.[1] For such a purpose a verbatim account would be desirable and the services of a shorthand writer invaluable. As well as this in the second half of the 16th century a quite different use for shorthand developed. Puritans were anxious to record what was said by their favourite preachers and, when they were able, so frequently used shorthand for the purpose that in some of the earlier systems there are special symbols for favourite texts and moral principles.

There was therefore by the end of the 16th century a demand for shorthand which resulted in the invention of a variety of systems. In 1602 John Willis produced an alphabetical system of shorthand which was quickly followed by a spate of other

[1] *State Trials*, Vol. I (1719), p. 66. David Jardine, *Criminal Trials* (1852), Vol. I, p. 143.

systems, a flood which went on into the century. In spite of these developments it would seem probable that the early 17th century shorthand writers were not very skilful. It has been proved with reasonable certainty that writers using the systems available would have been incapable of recording a performance of King Lear to provide for the quarto edition which appeared in 1608; indeed Sir Isaac Pitman, who was an expert, after reviewing all the systems of the first thirty or forty years of the 17th century came to the conclusion that it would not, for technical reasons, be possible for anyone using them to take down more than fifty to seventy words a minute whereas an ordinary public speaker utters about 120 words to the minute and a rapid speaker reaches about 180 to 200 words.[1] Nevertheless it is clear that the use of shorthand was spreading, and in due course was to gain some sort of official recognition. In 1640, for instance, John Rushworth was appointed Clerk Assistant to the House of Commons. Rushworth was a short-hand writer, and though he was forbidden to take notes except at the order of the House. he says of himself, 'I began early to take in characters [that is shorthand] Speeches and Passages at Conferences in Parliament, and from the King's own mouth, when he spake to both houses'.[2] In 1637, before his appointment, he had reported the argument of the Judges and Counsel in the case of Ship money. He was rather apologetic about this report afterwards, for he says of this case: 'of which the author gives the Reader a large account himself being then present, and took the Argument in Characters; yet begs the readers pardon for any mistakes, for it is not possible for a single pen to be so circumspect in mentioning so many Authorities of Books and Records, but that something may be misrecited or omitted, when his hand with so continual writing might sometimes grow feeble and thereby disinable him'. He also implies elsewhere that there were some things he could not hear.[3]

[1] George Ian Duthie, *Elizabethan Shorthand and the First Quarto of King Lear* (Basil Blackwell, Oxford, 1949). Sir Isaac Pitman, *A History of Shorthand* (4th edition, 1918), p. 23.

[2] John Rushworth, *Historical Collections*, Vol. 1 (1659). Preface (no page numbers).

[3] John Rushworth, *Historical Collections*. The Second Part (1680), p. 480 and Preface.

In spite of these difficulties the shorthand reporting of important cases in the law courts had come to stay. When King Charles the First was tried in 1649 a team of shorthand writers was organized by the government in order to gain a correct record,[1] and after 1660, shorthand writers were clearly becoming reasonably commonly accepted figures in the Courts at Westminster, indeed in 1683 during the trial of Sir Patience Ward for perjury the testimony of one Blaney, a shorthand writer, using his notes was admitted as evidence to what had been said in court on a previous occasion.[2]

Even so it would probably be a mistake to exaggerate the competence of shorthand writers at any date in the 17th century. Very great improvements were to be made in shorthand in the 18th century, and it must be assumed that writers who had not the advantage of these changes could not achieve the speed and certainty of late 18th or 19th century reporters. Indeed there seems to be evidence of the limitations of 17th century reporters. In this trial of Sir Patience Ward, Blaney seems to have been pressed hard in cross examination and to have been driven at last to confess, 'I don't pretend to say I have written down every word', and it seems to have been assumed by Counsel that he would not have done so.[3] Moreover in the period between the Restoration and Revolution complaints about the inaccuracy of shorthand seem to be common, though it has to be confessed these seem as often to reflect on the good faith of the writers as on their competence.

If however, as seems probable, the competence of 17th century reporters was a good deal less than what we are used to today it is impossible to avoid asking this question: what did the writers do when their skill was not equal to the task? The answer to this question must be hypothetical, but it seems obvious. Even using the efficient shorthand writers of today it is not normally possible that a speech can be published exactly as given; such is the general ruggedness of normal human speech that a certain amount of tidying up seems to be normally inevitable. If so the lacunae and the obscurities left by the far less effective 17th century systems of shorthand

---

[1] C. V. Wedgwood, *The Trial of Charles I* (1964), pp. 125–6.
[2] *State Trials*, Vol. V (1730), pp. 412–35.
[3] *State Trials*, Vol. V (1730), p. 421.

would mean that a more extensive reconstruction would be necessary, before a presentable account of such a thing as a trial could be placed before the public. After all men must have become used to accepting such reconstructions as inevitable when they had produced what appeared to be the coherent verbatim account of a trial before shorthand was invented at all.

Such a possibility however alters the nature of the document that may come to hand. Any extensive reconstruction of an incomplete report is likely to mean that a certain amount of material has been added from the imagination of the compiler in order to make sense. This will in effect not be what he knows was said, but what he thinks was probably said, or ought to have been said and, obviously, is likely to be coloured by his own point of view. But to people who are used to creating what appear to be verbatim accounts from incomplete notes this practice of supplying the gaps may appear to be so inevitable as not to seem to be particularly shocking. Indeed in all ages there have been people who have not been much impressed by the sacrosanct nature of what appears between inverted commas. To put a remark into direct speech into someone's mouth has always appeared to them to be a natural way of expressing what they believe he thought at any given moment, or of summing up his situation, whether he said anything of the sort or not. Probably this way of looking at things becomes more natural as the possibility of recording a verbatim account of what a man did actually say gets less. Certainly the further you go back in time the convention of what is implied by putting things into direct speech seems to change.

An obvious example of this is the practice among ancient historians of crediting important characters with speeches which sum up and dramatize a particular situation. This tendency also helps to resolve a problem I mentioned in an earlier chapter, the problem of what could be the possible evidence for some of the conversations and events reported in the Gospels. The question who reported the dialogue between Christ and Pilate in the Palace, or for that matter between Christ and the woman of Samaria at the well, disappears if it is true that the author of the Gospel was not pretending to record the verbatim account of an actual conversation, but rather to put forward important doctrine in dramatic form, to express the significance of a past situation and to fit all this into the realities of an accepted story. To compare great things with what is infinitely less, may not something of the same convention have affected those who took ragged notes and incomplete recollections and fitted them together to make a coherent story of an important trial?

The trouble begins when the convention is changed, when what has been written by people who were not deeply interested in literal accuracy passes into the hands of people who firmly believe that what they have is an exact account of what was said or took place. This is what has happened to the Gospels. What has been recorded in them has seemed so important and is in itself so vivid and heart searching that men and women have become passionately attached to a belief in the literal accuracy of every detail, not only as reported in the original Greek, but also, by a strange but significant extension, as translated into Latin or English. No doubt the nature of the Gospels puts them into a special class, but probably where any report is detailed and convincing and has been generally accepted there is a temptation to forget that it must be the work of a fallible human being, whose conventions about such things as direct speech may be different to ours, whose standards of accuracy may be questionable and who might even not be acting in good faith.

This may be true of anyone who has had a hand in producing a report. After all shorthand writers, and even editors, are men. They have their interests and passions like other folk, and they may be partisans. For instance Robert Blaney, the late 17th century shorthand writer mentioned earlier, was apparently a Whig. He was the son of a major in Major-General Massey's army in the civil war, and was himself examined for complicity in the Rye House plot. He was also accused of falsifying the reports of trials, both in general and specifically in the case of certain Roman Catholic priests who had been accused by informers of complicity with the Popish plot. In this case the accusation against Blaney seems to have been justified, but it would be difficult to guess how far his political connections affected his reporting. He seems to have been still employed by those who were not Whigs in 1684 after the episode of the Rye House plot, and since complaints of the inaccuracy of his reports were not only made by Roman Catholics and Tories but also by Lord Shaftesbury and the informers Bedloe and Oates it may be presumed that some of his failures derive from genuine incapacity, or more probably the limitations of his art at the time, rather than from partisan interests.[1]

Whatever the truth of this his example plainly demonstrates how dangerous it is to forget the human agents who must be employed before what happened in Court or Parliament can be translated into a printed account. Yet this is precisely what men are apt to do, and in order to realize how easy it may be to make this mistake it may be worthwhile to follow the history of the reports of English trials in the 16th and 17th centuries a little further and see what some 19th century historians made of them.

The collection from which these reports have usually been taken is sometimes called Cobbett's or Howell's *State Trials*, from the names of those who were responsible for them in the 19th century. The history of them however goes back to the beginning of the 18th century, to a collection of trials published in four folio volumes in 1719. New volumes were added in 1730, and thereafter new editors added other volumes with new trials and reprinted the other volumes without apparently editing them till the collection reached massive proportions in the 19th century. The collection is in no way an official publication. The word 'State' in the title only implies that the trials relate to matters of high public importance, which most of them do. Six names appear on the first page of the first edition as responsible for publication. According to Mr Muddiman the editor of the first volumes was a journalist called Thomas Salmon and of the supplementary volumes issued in 1730 was another journalist called Sollum Emlyn.[2]

It will be necessary to return to the questions, who was first

---

[1] J. G. Muddiman, *Notes and Queries*, Vol. 155 (1926), pp. 111–12, 'State Trials and Robert Blaney', and by the same author, *State Trials: the Need for a new and Revised edition of "State Trials"*. William Hodge and Coy Ltd, Edinburgh and London, 1930. It will be noted that these two accounts do not quite correspond, and it is presumed that the second is the more accurate. The first, however, contains matter not in the second.

[2] W. G. Muddiman, *State Trials* [op. cit. p. 92], pp. 5 and 6.

responsible for first making the collection, and in what way it was made. The point which is of importance here is that the collection has been very widely used. It has not only been used by historians, it has also been used by those who valued it for the excellence of the reading it provided, and the vividness of the pictures that emerge of contemporary manners and scenes. Thackeray took from the trials of Lord Mohun a large part of the account of the fatal duel in *Esmond*. In the same set of Essays as that in which he printed his study of Defoe, Leslie Stephen discusses the *State Trials*. 'The charm', he says, 'of the State Trials is in the singular fulness and apparent authenticity of the *viva voce* examinations'. 'The very words are given fresh from the speaker's mouth'; and he gives as his instance the report of the trial of Sir Nicholas Throgmorton, or Throckmorton, whose words he has in fact quoted a little earlier in the Essay.[1]

On one point Sir Leslie is unquestionably right, the long examinations in the *State Trials* are well worth reading. They are racy with the life of the times. Sometimes they are exciting, sometimes very moving, almost always do you feel that here at least you are in contact with real breathing, suffering, lying, truth telling, cowardly, courageous people who lived in the past and were for a moment exhibited in their reality by the haphazard actions of the law. The trial of Sir Nicholas Throckmorton, which Sir Leslie quotes, is a case in point. In 1554 in the reign of Mary Tudor he was tried on a charge of treason for complicity in Wyatt's rebellion. In the account in the *State Trials* he fights for his life against the best legal brains that the government can bring against him, through what must have been long, desperately anxious hours in the Guildhall in London where the trial took place. He shews great coolness and ability and, for a man who was confessedly not a lawyer, a surprising knowledge of contemporary law. And he wins. That part of the record is confirmed by other contemporary records. The Jury acquitted him to the great anger of the government, who fined the members of the Jury handsomely, for what was held to be a breach of their duty.

It is all extremely vivid. There remains however a teasing

[1] Sir Leslie Stephen, *Hours in a Library* [op. cit. p. 67], Vol. III, p. 288.

problem. How was it all recorded? An early 19th century
magistrate, David Jardine, who tried to collate the state trials
with contemporary documents left this note on Sir Nicholas'
trial: 'This report is taken entirely from Holinshed and is
very imperfect. Unfortunately there are no means of rendering
it more complete and intelligible; for no other account of the
proceedings is to be found. Nor are the examinations of the
several witnesses, nor of Throckmorton himself at the State
Paper Office'. In Holinshed's chronicle, in fact, the account
seems almost as if it were put in as an afterthought. After
describing Throckmorton's trial and acquittal, the wrath of
the government and the punishment of the Jury, Holinshed
says: 'But nowe for as much as a copy of the order of Sir
Nicholas Throckmorton's arreignment hathe come into my
hands, and that the same may give some light to the history
of that dangerous rebellicn I have thought it not impertinent
to insert the same'. This brings this account back to 1577 when
Holinshed published his book, there remain therefore twenty-
three years between 1577 and the date of the trial. Moreover
the first four years after it took place, that is till the accession
of Elizabeth, would not be propititious to any account of this
trial being preserved, least of all published, since the trial had
gone very much the wrong way for the government of the day.
Moreover the account in the *State Trials* seems to be slanted
in favour of Sir Nicholas who is credited in it with many
telling legal points and much piety of expression. If therefore
it existed in this form in those years, it would have been a
dangerous document to possess.[1]

This account however presents another fundamental problem: 'Who made a record of what happened in court and how
much did he record?' In the first edition of the *State Trials* it
occupies roughly fourteen folio pages printed in double
columns. It contains both longish speeches and quick exchanges.
The trial took place sixty or seventy years before any practicable
system of shorthand was available. If, then, this is in any way
a literal record of what was said, how was it recorded? No
doubt 16th century lawyers had better memories than we have

---

[1] David Jardine, *Criminal Trials* [op. cit. p. 87], Vol. I, p. 62. Raphael
Holinshed, *The Chronicles of England, Scotlande and Ireland* (1577), Vol. II,
p. 1,737.

and great skill in using abbreviations and making notes, but if recollections and notes were all that was available after the trial, a good deal of reconstruction surely must have been necessary before such a long, fluent, and connected account could be created out of them.

The trial certainly reads as if it were taken down verbatim. There is much convincing detail, the speeches are in vigorous and lively English, which reads like the language of real men. It has the ring of truth. It should, however, be remembered that so has the work of Defoe, and that the effect which Defoe produced by art could be brought about by accident, if enough detail has been remembered or supposed. Nor is the raciness of the language much guarantee of authenticity. In the same volume there is an account of the trial of Mary Queen of Scots. In it Mary's answers are often couched in language that has great vigour and life, yet Sir John Neale has shewn conclusively that in fact this account is an English translation of the Latin account by William Camden. The actual language is therefore that of an unknown translator and not of a Queen facing her fate.[1]

It is, of course, possible to speculate about the process by which the account of Throckmorton's trial came into being. It may very well have been reconstructed from the memories of people who had actually been present in the Guildhall at the time of trial, possibly assisted by their notes, possibly assisted by the recollections of Sir Nicholas himself. It may well have been issued early in the next reign, when the sufferings of the former times were being celebrated, as in Foxe's *Book of Martyrs*. It might have been issued partly as propaganda for the new régime. All this, however, is guesswork. What is not guesswork is that so intelligent a man as Sir Leslie Stephen, the first editor of the *Dictionary of National Biography*, said of this trial: 'The very words are given fresh from the speaker's mouth', and never asked how the words came to be where they were.

There is no need to press this too heavily against Sir Leslie. He was thinking in this article of the entertainment value of the *State Trials*, not of their use as historical evidence, though

[1] Sir John Neale, *Eng. Hist. Review* (1923), Vol. XXXVIII, pp. 443–6 (review of A. F. Stewart, *The Trial of Mary Queen of Scots*).

he clearly believed that their literal historical accuracy added to their entertainment value. What is important is that Sir Leslie's attitude suggests the compulsive effect which a vivid account of an event such as this trial, furnished with sufficient adventitious detail, confidently expressed, where that is suitable in direct speech, has on any man's mind. It does not banish doubts: it prevents them being raised. What it reports seems so obviously real and concrete that a man thinks no more of asking how the report came into existence than Sir Leslie Stephen asked of this trial.

In this case the questions which were not asked were largely those in the first group, those which arise from the question: 'How did these speeches and these exchanges come to be recorded?' With the trials in the late 17th century when the business of reporting is on a more regular basis perhaps the questions which are set in motion by the questions, 'How did these trials come to be collected and published', come more into prominence, though the first questions should never be forgotten. That period also has the advantage that it presents a minor historical problem which turns largely upon the validity of the evidence of reported speech. It is the problem of the true character of the infamous Judge Jeffreys, the Jeffreys of the 'bloody assize', the assize in the West in 1685 after the rebellion of the Duke of Monmouth against James II.

George Jeffreys, Lord Jeffreys of Wem, Lord Chief Justice in 1682, Lord Chancellor from 1685 to 1688 is one of the relatively few figures in British history who have found a secure place in popular mythology. Indeed mythology rather than history would seem to be the proper setting for the normal conception of him. The dreadful appearance on the bench— glowering and red, bleared from the drinking bout of the night before, now shouting foul abuse at the prisoner, now sancti- monious, using sacred names with an unpleasing familiarity, now indulging in horrible jocosities, but all the time using its great astuteness to drive the wretch to the gallows—seems to be something which has come in from outside humanity. In fact the myth has been partly derived from popular memory fairly heavily laced with contemporary, or nearly contemporary, propaganda and partly from the drastic account which Macaulay gave of Jeffreys in his great *History*.

In the last sixty or seventy years men have begun to wonder how far this picture corresponded with the Jeffreys of reality. Even if the picture was not to be revised it became clear that it had to be brought into focus, and in particular set against the conditions of the time, for many things which seem outrageous now were unfortunately habitual then. For one thing, whatever the Judge, the practice of the 17th century law was harsh. It was particularly savage where men and women were charged with high treason. As with everyone who was charged with felony they were denied the aid of counsel, and they were normally matched against the best legal intelligence of their day. They came into court often not fully aware of the case against them. The rules of evidence were but hazily recognized and evidence was accepted against them which would be excluded nowadays, and the law was fluid and was liable to be interpreted to their disadvantage. Moreover, Judges, other than Jeffreys, conceived that they had a primary duty to protect the King's government and the peace of the realm, and judges other than Jeffreys misbehaved in court and abused the prisoner, in fact there is contemporary evidence that Jeffreys could on occasion behave exceptionally well and had enlightened views about what ought to be the rights of accused persons. On the other hand there seems to be little doubt that on occasion he could be savage indeed.[1]

It is against the background of these conditions that Jeffreys must be judged. In addition it must be remembered that it was his plain unavoidable duty to do much that he has been blamed for doing. One must have every sympathy and great pity for the deluded countrymen who had come out with the Duke of Monmouth, but in the eyes of the law, they were without question traitors who had levied war against the King. Upon such, if the fact were proved, Jeffreys had no alternative but to pass sentence of death, after the horrible fashion of death reserved for traitors. It is true that the expedient adopted to expedite matters, that is of encouraging them to

---

[1] On Jeffreys' behaviour, W. S. Holdsworth, *A History of English Law*, Vol. VI (1924), pp. 527–30. G. W. Keeton, *Lord Chancellor Jeffreys and the Stuart Cause*, 1965, pp. 492–6. Arnold Lloyd, *Quaker Social History* (1950), p. 89. Testimony in Jeffreys Favour by Margaret Fox, wife of George Fox. Hon. Roger North, *The Lives of the Norths* (edition 1826), Vol. II, pp. 30–5.

plead guilty on the chance of life was not a pretty one. But it seems that Pollexfen, who accompanied Jeffreys as prosecutor, was the agent in this, though it had the assent of the Judges, and in any case it must be remembered that pretty well all the prisoners were in fact guilty and that it may be doubted whether any one lost his life through this practice who could otherwise have saved it. The number of those executed is distressing. Nevertheless in spite of what Macaulay says it is not clear that the vengeance taken after Sedgemoor was more severe than what Cromwell executed in Ireland, or the Hanoverians in the Highlands after Culloden; and for its severity the fault must largely lie with James II rather than Jeffreys, for Jeffreys could only pass sentence on those convicted, while James could have pardoned them and did not do so.

In cases that were more doubtful than those of Monmouth's followers, as for instance those of Algernon Sydney and of Dame Alice Lisle where Jeffreys' position has been challenged, it now seems to be the best opinion that the law was more often on his side than used to be conceded. But for long his views and decisions were not likely to receive fair treatment, for whatever may be the truth about him there is no question that Jeffreys was brutally libelled both in his lifetime and after his death. There were indeed those who had every reason to encourage the circulation of libels about him after his death, for he died in the Tower immediately after the Revolution while others who had served with him went on to have careers under the new régime. For instance Pollexfen who had prosecuted for him on the bloody assize, became a Judge in 1689, or Sunderland, who had been Secretary under James II, became a minister of William III. Such men were not likely to defend Jeffreys' memory; indeed it was convenient for them that he should carry the blame for what had happened, while they disclaimed anything that might connect him with them. It is possible that this is the reason for the disappearance from the State Papers of all letters to and from Jeffreys for the reign of James II. It looks as if some one had got access to the papers who thought he had something to hide.[1] It is also just possible that his desire to put the blame on Jeffreys accounts for the

[1] I owe the information about the disappearance of Jeffreys' letters from the State Papers to Professor Keeton.

production of a document for which Pollexfen may have been responsible which has done much to blacken Jeffreys' reputation, but to that I shall return later.

It is therefore not surprising that the most recent biographies of Jeffreys, Seymour Scholfield, *Jeffreys of the Bloody Assize* (1937), and G. W. Keeton, *Lord Chancellor Jeffreys and the Stuart Cause* (1965), take a more favourable view of him than the older writers did. But the case is still an open one. No man could afford to consider it without reading Professor Keeton's interesting and exhaustive work, but it may be doubted whether it can ever be satisfactorily settled. Much of the evidence is doubtful or missing, and whatever view is taken of Jeffreys there are awkward and inconvenient facts in the record to set against it. What seems abundantly clear is that the truth about him is more complex, and therefore more instructive and interesting, than the old legend of an hobgoblin would suggest.

Fortunately there is no need here to venture an opinion on the main issue. The problem here is not what kind of man Jeffreys was but the problems presented by the reports of trials which men have had to use in tackling that problem. Here however the case of Jeffreys presents a particular complication. The most eminent of the historians who have dealt with Jeffreys is Lord Macaulay, and he, at times, sat so loosely to his sources that the issue which his work tends to present is, not so much the nature of the evidence which he used, as the relationship of the image which he produced to any evidence that might have been available. Since however men and women have normally read Macaulay and neglected his sources that problem is important in its own right when one is dealing with the intermediaries through whose hands evidence has passed. It would be as well therefore to say something about it before turning back to the problems of reporters and editors.

Macaulay's account of Monmouth's rebellion and its aftermath reveals his descriptive powers at their most remarkable and his use of evidence at its most questionable. It is an account which has entered powerfully into other men's work; historical works, novels, plays, films have been founded on it so that most people have felt its impact, if not directly then at second, third or fourth hand. Nor is it easy even now to read it without feelings of indignation and pity springing up in one's mind. Indeed it is a useful exercise to read through the relevant section of Macaulay's history uncritically without considering the question of evidence and allowing the emotions it naturally excites free play. It is then worthwhile to consider what he did with his evidence.

Probably his worst lapse had nothing to do with Jeffreys. It was his wanton, but obstinate, identification of George Penne, a rascal who was engaged in the dirty business of the sale of pardons, with William Penn the Quaker, a much respected individual whom Macaulay took other occasions to traduce.[1] However Macaulay's description of Jeffreys also shews to what lengths he could go. He starts with a vivid physical description which suggest that he cannot have spared more than a cursory glance at the rather numerous portraits of Jeffreys which have survived. He then proceeds to exploit indiscriminately all the evidence that suits his purpose, mixing serious evidence with evidence which other historians would reject, or would in this case only accept with a certain amount of misgiving: that is the evidence of men who are patently untrustworthy together with the evidence of men who though respectable were Jeffreys' avowed enemies. Thus he accepts against Jeffreys, without any apparent reservations, the evidence of Burnet a political opponent who was apt to rely on partisan gossip, the evidence of Richard Baxter whom Jeffreys tried and who wrote, sometime afterwards, a confused, and in some points a clearly inaccurate, account of his own trial, the evidence of Roger North who had a grudge against Jeffreys who had been the successful rival of Lord Chancellor Guildford North's brother, and of John Tutchin, a friend of Titus Oates and a proven liar, who wrote Whig propaganda about the Bloody Assizes and Monmouth's rebellion, in which he had apparently been involved under an assumed name.[2]

The evidence is however not only used indiscriminately; it is also used selectively. Macaulay takes what he wants from the evidence leaving aside what is inconvenient. In this case

[1] John Paget, *The New Examen* (1934), p. 147 ff.
[2] On the character of Tutchin, see J. G. Muddiman, *The Bloody Assizes* (1929), passim.

he leaves aside anything at all that could mitigate Jeffreys' conduct, or even explain it except in the most odious terms. Such mitigations appear in other accounts as will be seen in the discussion of Jeffreys' cases by a man who condemned him; they do not appear in Macaulay. Jeffreys is not even credited with an occasional respectability of behaviour which other people have noticed, or with the remarkable ability as a lawyer which almost everyone else has seen in him.

These failures are interesting because they are probably the other side to Macaulay's great powers as an historian and may perhaps suggest a danger which may be implicit in other great imaginative historians. Between the reader of Macaulay and the evidence there is interposed Macaulay's powerful historical imagination. The reader gains great advantage from it. It interprets and illumes. But it is not always clear what evidence has guided the interpretation, and therefore what is being illumined. Probably Macaulay was himself unaware what evidence he was using. The process by which he assembled his *History* was largely an unconscious one. What appears to have happened was this. Macaulay read voraciously everything that he could lay his hands upon, in this case all that related to Judge Jeffreys and the Bloody Assize. He consigned what he read to his magnificent memory and allowed his powerful imagination and equally powerful prejudices to play upon it. As a result of this process his vivid picture was forged. Probably when he wrote he did not know from where he had accepted testimony, or what he had left out or altered; or, since he was not given to self criticism, to what extent his preconceived values had moulded the whole. Nor does he seem always to have returned to his documents to check what he had written.

But perhaps it is best to consider his habits in relation to one particular episode, which has the advantage that it is a trial the record of which is in the *State Trials* which raises in its own right an important problem about the nature of evidence. It is also interesting because Macaulay distorts a report which has always been very easily accessible, and which there was no need for him to modify in any way, since unmodified it could easily have been made to endorse the case against Jeffreys that he wanted to make.

The episode is the case of Dame Alice Lisle, an elderly lady, the widow of a Cromwellian Judge who was tried by Jeffreys at Winchester for harbouring rebels after Sedgemoor and was convicted and executed. As told in the *State Trials* her trial is a very dramatic affair. There is a vivid picture of it in Sir Leslie Stephen's article. The central point is the examination of Dunne, the man who had led the fugitives to Dame Alice's house, and who could alone say whether she knew what manner of men she was harbouring. Upon him her life depended. At first Dunne tried to prevaricate, and tell the story in such a way that it was impossible for her to have known who the men were. Then according to the account in the *State Trials* Jeffreys inflicted upon him what must be one of the most terrible examinations which any Judge has ever inflicted upon any witness in any English trial. It went on at intervals during the whole trial, through the day and into the night and was mainly carried on by Jeffreys. He stormed, he appealed, he used his great acumen to pick holes in Dunne's story. He cleverly interpolated the testimony of other witnesses who made it clear that Dunne was not telling the truth; he had a candle held close to Dunne 'that we may see his brazen face'. And in the end he got what he wanted, evidence sufficient for a conviction. Meanwhile according to a tradition recounted by Leslie Stephen the poor old lady, whom this was all about, had dozed off in the chair provided for her.[1]

Macaulay naturally made much of this trial. For his description of it he clearly went to the account in the *State Trials*. Indeed there is no other full account of the trial from which he could have supplemented it, so that his use of it is an interesting example of his methods of work.

The first point to be made about his presentation may be a small one. Macaulay accused Jeffreys of swearing from the bench. He says of Jeffreys that 'he stormed, cursed and swore in language which no well bred man would have used at a race or a cock fight' and later that 'the judge broke forth in a volley of oaths'. Now in the account in *State Trials* Jeffreys is unusually verbose and possibly unusually abusive. He certainly

---

[1] *State Trials*, Vol. III (1719), pp. 489–516. Stephen, *Hours in a Library* [op. cit. p. 67], Vol. III, pp. 302–3. Macaulay, *History of England*, (ed. 1869), Vol. I, cap 5, pp. 302–4.

says such things to Dunne as 'Jesu God! was there ever such a fellow in the world as thou art', 'Jesus God! there is no sort of Conversation nor human Society to be kept with such People as these are', and so on. But it may be doubted whether this is the kind of thing which the words which Macaulay uses would suggest to those who have not read the trial. Except as in the sentences quoted there is no blasphemy, and there is no obscenity. It would be a very ladylike cock fight that would be disturbed by the Chief Justice's language. But 'swearing and cursing' and 'volleys of oaths' gave the impression of Jeffreys which Macaulay wanted to convey and he described Jeffreys' language, and probably so remembered it, accordingly.

From a general historical point of view probably the worst characteristic of Macaulay's account of the trial is that he never tries to set it in its historical setting and suppresses those parts of the trial which might have enabled his readers to grasp it for themselves. He portrays Dame Alice's shelter of the two fugitives as if it were a mere piece of charitable hospitality to fugitives simply because they were fugitives, a protection which it was said she had extended to Cavaliers in their time of trouble. In fact it seems fairly clear that the two fugitives, Snelson and Hicks, came to her as a known sympathizer. They travelled a considerable distance to reach her. They sent a letter to her beforehand to assure themselves of a welcome, and then walked twenty-five miles through dangerous country to her house. Nor, after reading the account in the *State Trials*, is it easy to avoid the conviction that she knew whence they came and what they were. She claimed not to have known Snelson, which was probably true, and to have thought that Hicks was in trouble as a nonconformist minister who had been addressing unlawful conventicles. But considering the state of the country and the recent nature of the rebellion that explanation seems a little thin.

At any rate when the fugitives' letter arrived she behaved in so suspicious a manner that the man who had brought it, whom Dunne had employed and who was already uneasy about the whole matter, after sleeping on it, went and reported it to Colonel Penruddock, the magistrate who ultimately arrested Dame Alice and the fugitives. When Snelson and Hicks arrived with Dunne it seems clear from Dunne's story, as finally unravelled by Jeffreys, that she knew full well what was happening.

If, therefore, as she said she disapproved of the rebellion it seems from the record that she was willing to succour rebels. From the point of a reader in the 20th or 19th century this fact may seem to make no great difference. What we are likely to admire is the readiness to succour men in distress whatever they might have been. Many men in the 17th century would think very differently. These men were traitors and knowingly to comfort and aid traitors was to become yourself guilty of treason. After the Revolution her sentence was quashed on the grounds that Hicks, over whom she was condemned, had not yet been convicted; but it is the opinion of the best legal historians that that fact at that date made no difference.

It is difficult for us to realize how the crime of treason appeared to many men in the 17th century. It was a crime against God and man, the worst of crimes which comprised all other crimes. It was also a threat to that order which was necessary for civilized life and which was always in danger from lawless men and rebels. How narrow the margin of safety was had been demonstrated in the lifetime of many of those in Court, when the same party that had been in arms at Sedgemoor had been successful. They had subverted the Church and executed the Archbishop of Canterbury. They had destroyed the monarchy and executed the King. After the siege of Colchester they had shot the leader of the garrison. The loyal clergy had been driven out of their livings; those who had tried to do their duty to the King had suffered grievously in body or estate. Jeffreys' family had suffered; the father of Colonel Penruddock, who arrested Dame Alice and in truth seems to have treated her as well as he could, had been executed after an abortive revolt against the Commonwealth. Of course there was another side to all this; nor should it mitigate one's repugnance at the savagery which condemned an old lady to death for giving one night's hospitality to two fugitives. But it should be one of the first maxims of historical criticism that when any act is considered it is necessary to try to see what may have conditioned the minds of all the actors, and it should be impossible to judge such a trial without realizing how men's minds in the 17th century were weighted

by the memories of past danger and violence and the apprehension of future danger and violence to come.

It would be idle to expect Macaulay to have tried to do any
such thing when the feelings of those he did not favour were in
question. But, if he described the trial at all, he might have
been expected to give an account of the relevant facts on which
the trial turned. This he has not done. He has not described
those parts of the proceedings which support the case that
Dame Alice knew what she was about. He calls attention to
the cruel examination of Dunne, but does not say what its
object was. That however is the clue to the whole trial. Until
his story was exposed Dunne had tried to lie in order to cover
by his lies one who in the eyes of the law was probably guilty.
It may be that Jeffreys went to too great lengths to get at the
truth. It may be that it would have been better if Dame
Alice's 'guilt' had not been uncovered. But not to mention
what was at issue is to falsify the facts, for it makes it impossible
for the reader to judge for himself what is put before him.

This is probably Macaulay's worst lapse. But there are
others. For instance Macaulay says that when he was summing
up Jeffreys reminded the Jury that the prisoner's husband had
borne a part in the death of Charles I, a fact which he
says had not been proved and was irrelevant to the issue. He
does not say that, according to the report he himself was using,
it was Alice Lisle herself who had introduced the death of
Charles I, saying she had wept tears at it, that Jeffreys told the
court that a relative of hers had approached Jeffreys on the
subject to express anxiety lest prejudice on that subject should
work against her, and that what Jeffreys actually said on this
point was this: 'I will not say what Hand her husband had in
the death of that blessed martyr she has enough to answer for
of her own guilt; and I must confess it ought not one way or
other to make any ingredient into this case what she was in
former times'. Jeffreys did however say that her husband might
have been responsible for the execution of the father of Colonel
Penruddock, an impropriety Macaulay does not notice.

At the end of the trial Macaulay says that the Jury retired
and remained long in consultation and that Jeffreys grew
impatient. He says: 'He sent a messenger to tell them that, if
they did not instantly return, he would adjourn the court and

lock them up all night. Thus put to the torture, they came, but came to say that they doubted whether the charge had been made out'. According to the report in the *State Trials*, it is true Jeffreys certainly did express impatience with the Jury 'and' to quote, 'would have sent for them with an intimation that if they did not come quickly he would adjourn and let them lie by it all night; but after about half an hour's stay the Jury returned'. They then did indeed express certain doubts which Jeffreys answered sharply, after which they came to what was no doubt a very reluctant verdict of guilty.

Next day Jeffreys sentenced Dame Alice to the horrible sentence of being burnt alive that afternoon. This Macaulay imputes to an excess of brutality on Jeffrey's part, which was only prevented by the plea of the clergy of Winchester, a body whom Jeffreys dared not offend, for a postponement in the execution. He does not say that burning alive was the appropriate sentence for women convicted of treason and that Jeffreys had no alternative but to pass it, that it was apparently not unusual for sentences to be carried out on the day on which prisoners were sentenced, nor does he say that Jeffreys did in fact postpone execution for some hours and ordered pen and ink to be brought to Dame Alice and suggested that if she employed her time 'well' she might hear further from him deferring her execution. Presumably he wished for a plea for mercy possibly accompanied by a confession. Macaulay does not mention this hint. Neither Macaulay nor anyone else can know why Jeffreys responded to the plea of the clergy of Winchester. It may have been, as Macaulay says, because he did not dare to offend them, but it would have been as easy to say that he had only threatened her with immediate execution to get a confession, and that he had always intended to postpone the execution, as in fact he did, in order to give her time to make her plea to the King. This she did, but the King would do no more than change the sentence from burning to beheading.

Such is the nature of Macaulay's account, and in this day and age it may not seem to be worth powder and shot. Macaulay is an old-fashioned historian. He has been criticized often enough and it may seem to have been a waste of time and space to have put him to the question again. There are, however, two reasons why such an inquisition seemed worthwhile. Even if Macaulay is obsolete his faults are not. His errors suggest the way in which a vivid imagination and strong feelings can always modify something which is presented to them by the memory alone and which has not been checked by reference back to the evidence from which it was originally derived. This is a process which one can sometimes observe as having taken place in one's own mind if one compares what one 'has always remembered' with the source from which it came. The other point is this. This trial has always excited interest and very many people have accepted Macaulay's account of it without noticing the discrepancies between it and the account in the *State Trials* from which it was derived, in spite of the fact that copies of the *State Trials* have been generally available in every large library. This tendency not to trace something which is widely accepted to its obvious source is not obsolete; a great many mistatements, misrepresentations and misquotations which are current in politics and journalism nowadays owe their power to the fact that most people can be relied on never to look anything up.

So much for the relation between Macaulay's account of the trial of Dame Alice Lisle and the account in the *State Trials* which he was using; there remains the question of the relation between the account in the *State Trials* and what may have taken place in the Great Hall of the Castle at Winchester on 27 August 1685. Before however considering that question it would be as well to consider the work of another, and possibly more trustworthy commentator of Jeffreys and his cases, Sir James Fitzjames Stephen, the brother of Sir Leslie Stephen. Sir James was a distinguished judge, the author of an important book on evidence, and also of a standard history of the Criminal Law in which he had occasion to discuss a good many of the cases in which Jeffreys took a prominent part.

He seems to have started from much the same assumptions as Macaulay, for he takes it for granted that Jeffreys was a blackguard and a disgrace to his profession. He was also taken in, as was Macaulay, by John Tutchin's false account of the sentence he claimed to have received for a seditious libel. Nevertheless when dealing with other cases his opinion is less one-sided and more careful. He could see what Macaulay could never see, that there was at times something to be said for the things which Jeffreys did and the causes he promoted. In the case of Lord William Russell in which Jeffreys appeared as one of the counsel engaged, in the cases of Lord Algernon Sydney and in that of Titus Oates, in both of which Jeffreys was a judge, Sir James recognized the strength of the case for the crown, and on occasion some defence for Jeffreys' behaviour, while of the trial of Lord Delamere he says, 'the remarkable point in the case is that Jeffreys seems to have tried it with propriety and decency'. It is noticeable that in this case also Macaulay simply makes Jeffreys' behaviour the target of his accustomed and unmitigated abuse. In the case of Dame Alice Lisle, Sir James comments on the harshness of the sentence, and on the ferocity of Jeffreys' examination of Dunne quoting some of the more brutal remarks attributed to Jeffreys, but he does at least say what was the object and at least partial justification for that examination. He also cannot accept the validity of the plea that since Hicks had not yet been convicted Dame Alice was guilty of no crime in receiving him.[1]

As well as this in contrast to Macaulay Sir James is prepared to adopt a critical attitude to the evidence which he is handling. He recognizes for instance how unsatisfactory is the report of Baxter's trial, which Macaulay simply uses as a source of vivid narrative and telling quotation to be used against Jeffreys. Sir James is also interested in the way in which trials were recorded. He says of the trials between 1678 and 1688 that for the first time the trials were reported by good shorthand writers and concludes: 'The result is that it is still possible to follow with minute accuracy every word of the proceedings'.[2]

In fact three things are wrong with this sentence. First, reasonably good shorthand writers had been available before 1678. Secondly, such is the untidiness of human speech it is not generally possible that even with skilled 19th or 20th century reporting what is ultimately produced gives with 'minute accuracy' every word that has been said. Some tidying

---

[1] Sir James Fitzjames Stephen, K.C.S.I., D.C.p., *A History of the Criminal Law of England*, 3 vols. (1883), Vol. I, pp. 408–16, for Russell, Sydney, Oates, Delamere, Lisle. Vol. 2, p. 317, for Tutchin.

[2] Sir James Fitzjames Stephen [op. cit. p. 108], Vol. II, p. 314, on Baxter and Vol. I, p. 383, on shorthand writers.

and editing has normally been necessary and with the hazards of the clumsier shorthand systems of the late 17th century added the need for editing and amplifying must have been greater. Thirdly, this statement might lead to the dangerous fallacy that because shorthand writers were available therefore it can be assumed that shorthand writers were used to report every case whose record is important. Nevertheless the statement shews a realization of the problems of reported speech beyond the conception of the large number of people who simply assume that what they see recorded on a printed page is a record of what was actually said. Nevertheless he does not press this enquiry far enough. He shews some interest in the way the trials he is commenting upon were reported. He does not ask who promoted, collected and edited the *State Trials*, the collection from which like others he draws most of his material.

Those questions should have been asked, but they are not easy to answer. The preface to the first edition of the *State Trials* is unsigned, but as has been said on the title page the work is said to be printed in London for six printers or publishers. The important problem would seem to be which, if any, of these really promoted and controlled the venture. An answer was given to that question in 1930 by J. G. Muddiman, the editor of the *Trial of Charles the First* and of *The Bloody Assizes* in the *Notable British Trials* series and of a good many other shorter studies on the reports of trials and the men who reported them in the second half of the 17th century; Muddiman's knowledge of the relevant literature must have been very great. He is however an historian to be used with some caution, for he was a very strong partisan on the royalist or anti-Whig side. But his work is probably trustworthy when it is carefully documented as it seems to be in this case; some of his guesses and general comments seem to be off target.

His account is as follows. In 1930 he discovered in the obituary of one John Darby who died in 1732 a statement that it was he who had promoted the *State Trials*. Darby was one of the six men whose names are recorded on the title of the 1719 edition as promoters. He was a printer of Whig pamphlets. Between 1705 and 1707 he published a highly eclectic series of *State Tracts* to discredit the Stuart cause, and it seems probable that the collection of *State Trials* was conceived with the same object after the defeat of the Jacobite rebellion in 1715. According to Mr Muddiman, in 1716 Darby and others advertised for copies of trials of the period of James I to Anne, that is the period of the constitutional struggle. However a very large number of trials were sent in and it was decided to enlarge the collection to include the trials of earlier times. In order, however, to get the trials now available into four volumes some rather drastic abridgement was necessary and the first editor, J. H. Salmon, a journalist of rather various achievements, was chosen for the purpose. According to Mr Muddiman he cut the trials mercilessly, as can, so he says, be seen if a comparison is made between the versions appearing in the *State Trials* and earlier versions. The venture was successful, additional volumes were printed in 1730. Darby died in 1733 and the collection passed into other hands.[1]

It would of course be desirable for this account to be checked by someone who has leisure and opportunity to work over the literature Mr Muddiman has used. In particular it would be interesting to know to what extent Darby and Salmon mutilated the reports they received. Fortunately some points about the origins of the *State Trials* can be confirmed from the first edition itself without reference to Mr Muddiman. For instance the inclusion of some apologetic documents which are not trials seem to suggest that it is indeed a collection made originally with a Whig bias.[2] More important than this, in the preface to the first volume there is a statement which throws an important light on the origin of some of the trials, which is amplified by notes in the Tables of Contents in subsequent volumes.

For the trials fall roughly into three groups, presenting slightly different problems as evidence. First there are the accounts of trials drawn from chronicles or earlier writers such as Holinshed or Camden. These if printed correctly have the authority of the source from which they were drawn, which may not be very easy to estimate, particularly if it is a medieval source. Secondly there are reports which were pub-

---

[1] J. G. Muddiman, *State Trials*, [loc. cit. p. 92].

[2] E.g., *State Trials*, Vol. III, 'A defence of the Lord Russell's innocency,' etc.

lished separately immediately after the trial. Some of these may have suffered the editing and truncation which has been described by Mr Muddiman, but probably many of them have not been so treated, and if not they ought to be good authority in so far as the capacity for shorthand writing at the date of the trial could make a good report, for such versions may have been authorized by the Judge, and what is more important were published independently of the editors and at a time when recollections of the trial were fresh.

There remains however a third group which the promoters said had been submitted to them 'in manuscript', some of which they say in their preface 'have been perfectly buried in private hands' and 'are here brought to light'. These clearly present rather difficult problems. What was the origin of these manuscripts? Why and where have they been hid sometimes for thirty years since the trials took place? In what state did they reach Darby and his friends? In these cases, it should be noted, there is no exterior check, no known version other than which is presented in the *State Trials*. The promoters apparently recognized the difficulty for they claim: 'And as to manuscripts, such care has been taken to avoid all Mistakes that the Judges and counsel, who were concerned in such Tryals, and are living, have been attended with their several arguments, and have been pleased so far to encourage the Undertaking, as to correct whatever was amiss'. But this check is of no great value unless one knows how it was made, and could be of no value at all when all the principal actors were dead. In any case a man's memory of what happened thirty years before may not be very reliable.

It is probably significant that of the cases which make up the gravamina of the charges against Jeffreys, several fall into this group. It is important not to press this matter too far. It is not quite true, as Mr Muddiman suggests, that all the accounts of all the trials in which Jeffreys is portrayed as a 'swearing and a railing bully' were not published till a generation after his death. There are intemperate expressions in accounts which were published at the time, particularly perhaps in the trial of Sir Samuel Barnadiston for seditious libel in 1685 which he himself authorized. Nor is it necessary to believe that the accounts of trials which do not appear before 1719 either are necessarily spurious, or have been tampered with. Nevertheless it is necessary to remember that for the integrity of these trials there is no outside evidence, that this was a period when the use of faked documents in party warfare was pretty common, that the accounts of all the trials in which Jeffreys appears to some advantage seem to be contemporary and that many of the trials in which he appears at his worst appear after a generation in unexplained manuscripts which have passed through the hands of his enemies. One of these trials is the famous account of the trial of Dame Alice Lisle.

In the 'Catalogue of the TRYALS contained in the Third Volume' at the beginning of that volume in the 1719 edition, it is described as 'The Tryal of the Lady Alice Lisle for High Treason, published from the Manuscript'. There is nothing in the printed trial itself to suggest its origin, but the pagination in the volume is strange. The trial runs (after the first page) from 490 to 516, each page having an asterisk by the number unlike any of the other pages in the volume, and it is inserted between pages 576 and 577. Mr Muddiman thinks that this was because it was an afterthought inserted after the volume was made up, but in fact the pages before 576 run up to 487 in the trial of Titus Oates and then jump to 576 on the last page of that trial so that something had gone wrong before this trial was reached, and there may be some other bibliographical reason for these vagaries. Leaving this minor problem out of account, however, the report still presents obvious difficulties. The trial took place on 27 August 1685 so that it must have remained in manuscript for thirty years or more, if it was put together at any date when the trial was at all recent. The last of the people principally involved in the trial, Pollexfen, died in 1691, so that if those who were responsible for the publication did make the kind of check that they claim to have made in the preface it can only have been with junior counsel, if any of these survived. If made it is unlikely that it was of great value so long after the event.

It would be idle to seek for the manuscript, or to ask who compiled it, or what materials he used, or why it remained unpublished for so long. Mr Muddiman believed that it was taken down by Blaney the shorthand writer whom he distrusted, but he could find no evidence to support this belief.

As a matter of fact there would seem to be no reason to assume that it was taken down in shorthand at all. As has been seen coherent accounts of trials were produced before the use of shorthand. If the trial had taken place in London it could probably be assumed that for a trial of this importance a shorthand writer would be present, but it can be guessed that it would less likely for such writers to be ordinarily available at Winchester. On the other hand it might very easily have been reported by someone who had followed the judges on what was likely to be a notable circuit, or by a barrister who knew shorthand.[1]

Anything else about this report must be based on supposition, but there seem to be certain likely suppositions. The first of these is that this account is at least based on notes which someone actually took down at the trial. There are in fact other accounts of this trial which are inconsistent with this one, but they are vague and it seems likely that they were founded on rumour. This report is detailed, succinct and intelligible and it seems likely that it is based upon some sort of record of what actually happened in court. It is true that this argument might seem to be an acceptance of the 'ring of truth' argument as evidence of authenticity and it is always important to remember how effectively Defoe for one could simulate the 'ring of truth'. Nevertheless considering the general nature of the report the assumption that it was based on something taken down at the time seems to be a reasonable hypothesis. This hypothesis however would only seem to cover what might be called the bones of the trial; it does not seem to cover all the words used. Here indeed the probability seems to swing the other way. A comparison between the style attributed to Jeffreys at this trial and his style in better authenticated reports, as for instance in the trials of Algernon Sidney and Titus Oates, suggests a considerable difference. In this trial he is more verbose, more emotional, less dignified and restrained and more generally abusive. Such a change indeed might be the result of the exigences of a particular situation—the challenge of a difficult case, the need to make an example in a matter on which something he is reported as saying at the trial suggests

[1] On the report of the trial of Dame Alice Lisle, see J. G. Muddiman, *Notes and Queries*, Vol. 155 (July–Dec., 1928), p. 111 and pp. 149–50.

he thought was a wide conspiracy, or it might be the result of Jeffreys' physical condition, since it is probable that Jeffreys was suffering severely from the stone at that moment. But it also might easily have resulted from someone having got hold of an account of the trial and filled it out with speeches that were intended to shew the temper of Jeffreys and his principles and his prejudices, and it is my own belief this is what has happened.

It is not easy even to guess who may have been responsible for the various stages of the report. It has been suggested that Pollexfen may have supplied notes on the trial. If this were so it might explain a minor mystery. In the account the examination of Dunne is attributed almost wholly to Jeffreys whereas it would have been natural that more of it would have been in the hands of Pollexfen the prosecuting counsel. It is supposedly possible that after the Revolution Pollexfen might have found it convenient to transfer to Jeffreys passages which he did not wish to have remembered against himself. But there is no sort of evidence for this. Pollexfen died very soon after the Revolution and there is no evidence that he had it in mind to publish this document to defend himself.

There are in fine no certain answers to the questions which this report raises. For present purposes, however, that fact is not nearly so important as the fact that normally these questions have not been asked. This is of more immediate significance than the reputation of a judge who has been safely dead for more than two and a half centuries. The problem of the nature of this report need not have waited for the suggestions of Mr Muddiman's discoveries; it is inherent in the report itself, particularly in the way it is introduced in the first edition of *State Trials*. Yet a very large number of people have simply assumed that this is a literally accurate verbatim account of what happened at Winchester, and have started their work from that point. Of the scholars I have mentioned, perhaps it is most surprising that Sir James Fitzjames Stephen failed to question the authenticity of this report, for he was a man with a powerful and critical mind, who in this very matter of the behaviour of Judge Jeffreys shewed that he could resist, at least in part, the sorcery of Macaulay, which was no easy matter in the 19th century.

It would be wrong, however, to accuse Sir James of any unusual failure in this matter. It is more healthy, as well as more realistic, to realize that in accepting the report as he did he was acting under the influence of compulsions which affect most of us most of the time. There is the compulsion not to question documents which are already generally accepted. There is the compulsion to be impressed by the evident truth of a detailed and comprehensive narrative, and there is the simple compulsion to accept what is presented on a printed page because it is on a printed page, a compulsion which is stronger with most people than they would care to admit. It is for this last reason that it is important always to remember the tedious questions, which I have suggested, about the various stages in the process by which anything is able to reach the printed page.

If those questions must be asked of any evidence which purports to have its origins in the spoken word, they are also relevant to evidence which purports to come from a written document. Before a document reaches the hands of an ordinary member of the general public the original is likely to have been copied by someone either for transmission as a manuscript or to go to the printers. Of course in the days before printing this was liable to happen a great many times over, as the material passed from scribe to scribe, and the whole elaborate and delicate science of textual criticism has been invented to deal with the errors which can creep in in this process. The invention of printing has diminished the possibilities of error from this source but has by no means brought them to an end. A printed manuscript must at least have been copied once, that is by the printers. If it is an historic document it may have been copied at least twice since it is unlikely that an original would be sent to the printers, though nowadays a photograph might be sent. Each time it is copied there are possibilities of error however great is the care which has been taken to avoid them.

When handling any printed document, therefore, it is desirable to keep the possible errors of copyists at the back of one's mind—words misread, words omitted, on occasion the epitome of a few lines which comes to be included as if they were the words of the original, or false rationalizations of what was not understood. But when considering such documents it is more important to realize the probable enormities of those who may have edited them, for it is from them that the most serious deceptions are likely to come.

A man who prepares as editor any material for publication —the text of someone else's work, a collection of official documents, a collection of someone's letters—ought to follow certain well-known rules, which make clear the relationship between what he prints and the original. The editor, for instance, must make clear in what hand a document is written, whether it is an holograph, that is written throughout in the hand of the supposed author, or a copy in another hand. If the editor leaves out words he must shew that he has done so by placing stars or dots in the text. If he supplies words— dates, names, words omitted—he must make it clear that such words are not part of the original text. He must always print what is in the original manuscript and not what appears to him to make clearer, better or more desirable sense. Any emendation he may wish to make should be presented for what it is and not as part of the text. Material should be printed in the order in which it appears in the original, or if that order appears to be misleading it should be clearly stated in what way it has been changed.

Unfortunately eminent editors have not recognized the importance of these rules and there is not one that has not been broken in important editions that are now in common use. Perhaps some examples may make this point clear.

The much used Everyman edition of John Locke's *Two Treatises of Government* was printed from an early edition which left out paragraph 21 in the Second Treatise. The editor took no account of this and went on with his enumeration taking 22 as 21, and numbering each paragraph one short of what it was in the original edition till he reached 35, which should of course have been numbered 36. At this point however it seemed for some reason to be desirable to get into step again. The editor did not however go back to the point at which the error started, explain what had happened and renumber from that point, which was what he ought to have done. He cut 35 in two at an arbitrary point, left out an 'and', and numbered the second half 36. This means that all references from other editions to any paragraph between 20 and 36 will be misleading and vice versa.[1]

A good example of the bad editing of important 19th century correspondence can be found in two collections of published letters, one from the papers of Sir Robert Peel and the other from those of Sir James Graham, each edited by the same man C. S. Parker.[2] These books were my first experience of the sins of editors when I was a young man engaged in historical research, and they came as a great and salutary shock. Parker often leaves out long and important passages from the letters he prints without giving any sign that he had done so, sometimes slightly modifying the syntax of what is left to hide the excision. He sometimes takes a paragraph from one part of a letter and puts it elsewhere because it seemed to him to make better sense. He can conflate two letters because they seem to him to be on the same subject. He can supply a date, which he had guessed, to an undated letter as if it were part of the original, and on one occasion at least it was a whole year wrong.

But Parker was not, in the 19th century, alone in his wickedness, and it may be as well to give another example which is the more remarkable because the offender is a Cardinal. Cardinal Gasquet was responsible for an edition of the letters of the great Roman Catholic historian Lord Acton. The letters, which are at Downside Abbey, have been compared with Gasquet's edition by Dom Aelred Watkin and Professor Butterfield. Their results are remarkable. The edition is incomplete. At least 200 letters have been omitted, some of great interest, a fact of which Cardinal Gasquet gives no hint. There are considerable lacunae in the letters which are printed. These are sometimes revealed by the interposition of dots, and sometimes not revealed. Different letters are conflated into one, and dates which were missing have been supplied. Words have been altered. Indeed it is calculated that of 163 letters printed in the book and discoverable at

---

[1] Peter Laslett, 'The 1960 Edition of Locke's *Two Treatises of Government*: Two States'. *Transactions of the Cambridge Bibliographical Society*, 4 (1952), p. 342, n. 2. (Mr Laslett drew my attention to this.)

[2] *Sir Robert Peel from his private papers edited for his trustees by Charles Stuart Parker* (3 vols.) (1899.) *Life and Letters of Sir James Graham* (2 vols.) (1907.)

Downside only 13 have been produced as written. Many of the changes were clearly deliberate. Cardinal Gasquet seems to have wanted to save space and to avoid trouble with living people, both in their way quite legitimate motives if, when acting upon them, the editor makes it quite clear what he has done, as Cardinal Gasquet did not do. He also clearly wished to preserve the proprieties. Acton from time to time refers to Cardinal Newman as 'Old Noggs', this Gasquet habitually turns back to the more decorous 'Newman', without of course revealing that he has made any change.[1]

Against this kind of thing the ordinary reader of history has no defence. He is unlikely to be able to go back to the original documents to check what has been done, and the editions of documents in which these tricks have been played, and the editions of documents, of which there are many, in which the rules have been observed, appear exactly alike as presented to the general public. It could be wished that the rules of good editing were generally taken more seriously than they are, and that more people should make it their business to stigmatize publicly those editors who have failed to observe them. But as things are, the only advice that can be given is: 'Be on your guard'.

As a matter of fact the ordinary user of history is probably less concerned with documents that are published in collections than with the evidence upon which historians and others have based the work which they present to him, for this is the closest point of contact that most people have with historical evidence.

In many cases it is not really a point of contact at all. If a writer—an historian, a journalist, a politician or whom you will—simply makes up his own mind about the evidence and gives the results dogmatically to the public, then he personally stands wholly between his readers and the evidence, and they are faced with the simple choice of either believing or disbelieving him. They can pass no judgement on the evidence for themselves. In certain cases there may be no alternative to the presentation of a report in this way, but it should be recognized how unsatisfactory it is, particularly when it is the

[1] Dom Aelred Watkin, O.S.B. and Professor H. Butterfield, 'Gasquet and the Acton-Simpson Correspondence', *Cambridge Historical Journal*, Vol. X, No. 1 (1950), pp. 75–104.

work of a journalist of whom one knows little filtered through the control of a sub-editor of whom one knows less. All concerned may be both intelligent and honest, but it is not desirable to have to rely so absolutely on other people whose standards of accuracy and scholarship one has no means of checking.

Nevertheless in almost all cases it will be necessary to rely at some point on someone other than oneself. If something is produced with the full apparatus of scholarship—notes giving references for all the important statements, a critical discussion of sources, a careful statement of the grounds for any decision that may have been made on any difficult question which the evidence may have presented—the reader will be in a much better position to judge for himself than if these things have not been provided for him, but he is still likely to be completely dependent in more matters than he may care to think on the writer having played fair and worked accurately. However detailed the references it is idle to suggest that the ordinary reader is going to look them all up and check them with the originals to see that they have the meaning which is imputed to them. If the book is in the main stream of historical scholarship then it is probable that it will be tested sometime by other scholars working in the same field, and sometimes a conscientious reviewer will check a selection of the references to a book, in order to judge the author's methods. But it is largely a matter of chance whether this is done. Often it cannot be done. Where for instance the evidence is in some closely guarded private collection, or in an outlandish place, it is possible that it will never be checked. But even if this is not so, it is not possible for scholars to reconsider and check all the evidence used by other scholars. If they felt called upon to do so the wheels of scholarship would grind to a halt. Scholars must in some matters take other people's work as a starting point, and when they do this they are like everyone else completely dependent on the integrity, accuracy and critical capacity of the people whose work they use.

But if such dependence is inevitable it is important that it should be recognized and acknowledged. It is important that everyone should recognize to what extent they are irrevocably dependent on other men's standards of honesty and accuracy.

It is highly important that writers should acknowledge their dependence on other writers. For this reason if a quotation is used, or if evidence is cited, it is important that reference should be made not only to its ultimate but to its immediate source, so that a writer may not appear to base his statement on an original, of which in fact he knows nothing, when in truth he is using another man's version of the original. This is not only a matter of common honesty, for a man should give other men their due and not pretend to knowledge he does not possess, it is also necessary to avoid misrepresentations and misconceptions. For as a reference or a quotation gets further from the original the more likely it is to be misinterpreted and misunderstood and it is important to know how far you have to go back before you reach someone who has actually seen the quotation in its context.

Unfortunately this rule is by no means always adhered to. Sometimes writers have taken the reference out of another man's footnote and cited it as if it were their own, when in fact they have never referred to the original from which it came. What is more common is for writers to draw a fact or quotation from another man's work because it suits an argument, or a description, and cite it as if it were drawn from their own knowledge, when in fact they do not know enough of its context to understand its original significance or meaning. All these practices are to be deplored. The lifting of another writer's reference without acknowledgement and without any attempt to go back to its source is a serious offence against the ethics of scholarship. It can at times be detected by those who know the relevant documents well; it is very difficult for those who do not know them to realize what may have happened. However this offence is more likely to matter to scholars than to the ordinary user of history. What will matter to *him* are the facts which are confidently cited but which if they were once set against their proper background would never support the arguments which they are supposed to support, or the quotations used, with an apparent familiarity with their origin, which, however, if restored to their right context would never bear the meaning which is imputed to them. It is very worthwhile to trace some favourite phrases and instances to their sources in order to realize how misleading such things often are, where men have appropriated other men's knowledge without saying what they are doing, or fully understanding what they are taking.

Unfortunately it is not possible to check everything; it is only possible to remember that ideally everything ought to be checked. It is however possible and desirable to view with the profoundest suspicion the debased currency of convenient facts and suitable quotations which reappear time and time again in the pages of writers who cannot know where they come from. It is, quite soberly, a reasonable assumption that anything which has got into currency in this way has changed its significance and meaning, that what has been, ignorantly, quoted three times is untrue—or at least does not have the meaning attributed to it.

It is therefore probable that any report about past events, or words spoken in the past, may have passed through the hands of one or more of these intermediaries, the reporter, the editor, the historian—whoever, scholar, journalist or general narrator—is acting as historian. They are all human beings, and it is important to remember that their failings, passions and interests as human beings may have affected what they have passed on and try to take that fact into account when considering the evidence. This is likely to be most difficult in the case of the historian. In the case of the reporter and the editor there is a definite objective fact behind the intermediary —the speech as it was originally delivered, the event which the reporter described, the document upon which the editor worked. This fact may not be recoverable, but it is often possible to work out the relationship of the intermediary to it in fairly simple objective terms. What lies behind the historian is likely to be more complicated. It is likely to be in fact a mass of disparate evidence which the historian has welded into a unity. This introduces into the final result a much larger element of human judgement than in the work of a reporter or an editor, and it is not easy to apply decisive objective tests to the use of human judgement. Historic judgement may be used with scrupulous and systematic fairness, or it may be used loosely and under the influence of strong personal feelings as in the case of Macaulay; only the effect of bias and the failure of the critical faculty may not be so easy to detect as they are in Macaulay.

Macaulay is, however, a good example in so far as he shews clearly how the brilliant work of an historian may interpose itself between the user of history and the evidence on which history rests. It has, however, been suggested that Macaulay is not relevant to the needs of this generation, that he wrote before the revolution in history writing, which was initiated by Von Ranke, and that what men and women are likely to consider will in all but a few cases be based on a much more scrupulous use of evidence. This ought to be so, but I am afraid as things stand it is a dangerous delusion, particularly if you take into account the very large amount of important and influential history which is not written by professional historians. In order to clinch this matter I think it is worthwhile to examine the methods of another popular historical writer who had very great influence in this century and also strayed from his evidence. He is Lytton Strachey, the author of the widely read book *Eminent Victorians*, two passages in which have been fortunately studied and criticized by two scholars working separately. Lytton Strachey wrote forty years ago, but in choosing him it should be understood that I am guided by the availability of these two excellent criticisms. There is every reason to believe that the same kind of criticism could be applied to historical writers who have died more recently, or who are alive today.

The first of Strachey's critics is Dr Bernard Allen. He dealt with Strachey's essay on General Gordon. Strachey wished to portray Gordon as a heavy drinker. The only evidence that could be produced for this was a certain amount of fugitive and malicious gossip, hotly denied by his friends. Since Allen wrote a little additional evidence has turned up on the point, but this seems to be also ultimately founded on gossip and may very well be a case of 'unreal corrobation'. Be that as it may what Strachey possessed was not enough for his purposes; to endorse it he therefore quoted from a description of Gordon by Richard Burton, who admired Gordon, a sentence which Strachey had removed from its context and so made to mean something quite different from what Burton had plainly intended it to mean. To clinch the matter Strachey told a story which he had drawn from the work of one, Chaillé-Long, who had been in the Sudan with Gordon. Chaillé-Long was a bitter critic of Gordon and was also well known to be an unreliable writer. It is difficult to prove a negative, but Dr Allen proves beyond reasonable doubt that the story Chaillé-Long told never could have had any foundation in fact. Apart from that Chaillé-Long told the story twice and on the second occasion considerably altered the details of the story from what he had told on the first occasion. It is this second, even more questionable, version of a story which in any case was probably fabricated which Strachey used to back up his insinuation that Gordon was a heavy drinker. Even so in order to make his point he had to modify and sharpen the details. With this in mind it is instructive to read Strachey's elegant and convincing account of the matter and then to turn to Dr Allen, in order to learn how effectively evidence can be perverted.[1]

The other scholar is the Rev. F. A. Simpson who criticized Strachey's study of Cardinal Manning. Strachey wishes to portray Manning as pre-eminently a worldly and ambitious man. A serious obstacle to this enterprise was the fact that at the age of forty-three, with a brilliant career in the Church of England opening before him, for the sake of conscience Manning had thrown it all up for an unknown future in the Roman Catholic Church. Strachey turned this difficulty by suggesting that before he went over Manning had been promised preferment by the Pope, Pius IX.

The way Strachey did this is well worth considering. In 1848 Manning, still an Archdeacon in the Church of England, had an audience with Pius IX. Strachey makes a mystery of this interview. He says: 'Precisely what passed on that occasion never transpired', and he mentions as the only point that was known one detail which clearly he thought to be ludicrous. This however is a misrepresentation. Manning left on record in various places a full account of the interview and of the object of the interview. And not only are these things known, but Strachey must have known them, for he used the books which contained them, indeed he used the page opposite that on

---

[1] Lytton Strachey, *Eminent Victorians* (1924), p. 209 ff. Bernard M. Allen, *Gordon and the Sudan* (1931), pp. 82–101.

which an essential part of the account can be found. Having, however, created this mystery Strachey was in a position to use it when describing Manning's conversion to Roman Catholicism in 1851. When he came to that point he suggested that at this mysterious interview, Pio Nono had told Manning that he would look after him if he became a Roman Catholic. The extreme improbability of the Pope making such promises to a strange Protestant clergyman, or making them with such assurance that an ambitious man would stake his future upon them and the fact it is not even pretended that there is any evidence that anything of the sort took place, are obscured in men's minds by the feeling which Strachey had created that something had happened in 1848 which needed explanation, and therefore that the explanation he gave was in the circumstances a likely one. From that point he can gently press home his insinuation that when Manning left the Church of England he knew that his future was assured in the Church of Rome.

Again it is well worthwhile first to read Strachey's account and then Mr Simpson's extremely penetrating criticism to understand how effectively Strachey based a case on evidence which does not exist.[1]

[1] Lytton Strachey, *Eminent Victorians* (1924), pp. 1–114. F. A. Simpson, *Cambridge Review*, Vol. 65 (4 December 1943). It could be wished that Mr Simpson's article was to be found in a more easily available form than in the columns of a weekly journal.

10

The Scholarly Attitude

THE CONCLUSION of these problems concerning the facts of history would then seem to be this. A framework of unquestionable fact covers, after some sort, a large area of human affairs. Unless for some philosophical reason all knowledge is uncertain, the knowledge of these facts is certain. It has never covered the whole field of human affairs, and as you go further back into history the spaces in the lattice work get larger. Though the main members of the framework are by definition unquestionable it must always be a matter of dispute and judgement how far it extends, and there are also in the history of any period disputable facts, likely guesses and probable hypotheses about facts which are not sustained by it.

The nature of human motive can never be guaranteed by the framework of fact, nor probably can the results of human action or of events, since it is not possible to know with certainty what would have happened if the facts had not been as they were. Nor is it possible to be sure that you know, or at least you know completely the causes of things. For this reason the framework of fact will never by itself supply the interpretation of history, though any interpretation that disregards the framework of fact can itself be disregarded.

Into the consideration of anything which lies beyond the framework of fact the human element will intrude. This is obvious in relation to any question of interpretation, but it is also true of any question of disputed fact. It will be necessary to take into account the extent and limitations of the powers of human beings to observe, to form inferences from what they observe, to remember, to record, to present what they have recorded in a newspaper or history book. But not only will the powers of human beings to observe, infer and record be in

question, but also the ways in which they do these things will
be controlled by their wills, by their passions, by their interests
and by the very fact that they are human beings.

All this will produce uncertainty, but there will be degrees
of uncertainty. The question with what degree of uncertainty
a fact should be accepted will provide problems to be resolved
by the use of trained judgement and the teaching of an experience of the problems which history presents. That judgement
and experience will without doubt suggest that much of what
human beings accept as part of their picture of the past is
spurious, or doubtful, or unknowable. But they will also
suggest descriptions and explanations of historical events which,
though tentative and hypothetical, are probably a better guide
to reality, and a surer basis for action, than what is proposed
by the confidence of ignorance.

Unfortunately it is not normally possible for the ordinary
user of history to press home himself the questions which ought
to be asked of evidence into which the human element has
introduced this element of uncertainty, or to resolve the problems which history presents. He may not have the skill and
experience to do these things; he will probably not have the
lesiure; he will almost certainly not have command of the
necessary material. Yet it is of considerable importance that
he should understand the rudiments of historical criticism.
He is after all the consumer. It is for his use that history and
journalism is written. If he demands a high critical standard
in what is written for him he will in the end get it. If he objects
that questions have not been asked of the evidence which
should have been asked, in due course those who are in a
position to ask such questions will make it their business to
do so.

In order to press home his legitimate requirements it is
however necessary for the ordinary reader to learn more than
he normally knows today about the techniques of scholarship
even if he is not going to use them. For instance it is important
that more ordinary unprofessional readers should understand
the significance of footnotes than now seem to do so. Footnotes
are not as many people seem to think the mere exuberance of
pedantry, and they ought not to be, as they sometimes are, the
tiresome reflections of an exhibitionist desire to parade erudi-

tion, or the result of an incurable diffuseness of mind. They should indicate, and when they are properly constructed they do indicate, the necessary links between the work of the historian and the evidence upon which it is based. Even if a reader has no chance to turn back to any of the documents cited he can learn much by letting his eye run over the footnotes of a work he is reading. He can see what kind of evidence the author is using to substantiate the statements he is making, whether it is someone's memoirs, a diary, private letters, public documents or whatever else it may be. He may guess whether his sources are likely to be one-sided, whether for instance he is taking his evidence too exclusively from the letters of one man and his circle, whether he is relying too much on obvious gossip and perhaps whether he is going back to original documents or whether he is relying on edited collections the accuracy of which may be questioned; and he may even form an opinion whether a reference can support the conclusions based on it. But none of these things can be learnt by a reader who has never learnt what a footnote is intended to do, and the rules which it ought to observe. Unfortunately many people, to judge by their comments, regard a formal footnote at the bottom of a page as a tiresome intrusion at which they have trained their eyes not to look, and are pleased when the notes are placed at the end of a book where they need not bother about them.

Scholarly writing demands scholarly reading and scholarly readers. Scholarly readers will demand a higher standard of scholarship in what is written for them, and higher standards of scholarship probably means a nearer approach to truth on matters which may be of considerable importance to mankind. But more important than any grasp of scholarly technique is the lesson of the habit of scholarly hesitation, the habit of the mind which teaches the great difficulty, even the impossibility, of arriving at the truth about many of the facts relating to events in the past. It is a habit of mind which leads to the rejection of much, and possibly the assured acceptance of little, but it can be used to dissolve for ever some of the legends, the dogmatic statements, the facile explanations which have troubled mankind,

Therefore the lesson of historical criticism as applied to the facts of history is to a large extent a lesson in how to doubt what perhaps might have been accepted previously without question. But it teaches doubt not scepticism, an uncertainty about what is to be accepted as truth not a belief that anything might be true or that everything may be false or that knowledge is impossible. The exercise of historical criticism does not teach blind doubt, doubt that does not discriminate between the degrees of certainty and probability, but rather trained or skilled doubt, that has learnt from man's experience to make this discrimination.

To learn how to doubt should therefore be one of the important rewards of an historical education. It is one key to what should characterize the attitude of the critical historian. I wish to devote my last chapter to a summary of that attitude. However before I reach that I wish to turn to one further historical problem. Hitherto what I have discussed has been concerned with the individual actions of particular men and women. In my next chapters I want to turn to the problems presented by generic statements about large numbers of men and women, or of events, or of facts, taken together. History would be meaningless without these generic statements, but they present some very difficult problems.

11

Generic Statements

By a *generic statement* I mean a statement about the common characteristics or behaviour of individual people, events or things, who are in some way joined into a group. It is an ugly phrase but I wish to use it rather than the word 'generalization' which might introduce other meanings. It might, indeed, open the door to the controversy whether generalizations and general laws are possible in history, which raises issues which seem to have little to do with what I want to discuss in this chapter.

Generic statements are often made by historians when they discuss the past, and often enough when ordinary people make generic statements about things in the present they are in fact making assumptions about what has happened in the past. As I said earlier on men and women are constantly making statements which depend upon, or are at least coloured by, opinions about history without being aware of the fact. Indeed an example which I gave then can be applied here. When a man talks about the common characteristics of the Germans, as a large group in the modern world, he is likely to be drawing upon the knowledge, or what he believes to be his knowledge, of the behaviour of the Germans in the past, though he may not realize what he is doing.

I shall return to the Germans, but I want to start with another kind of statement. The simplest and most obvious of the generic statements which are used by historians are those which enable history to be divided into periods, and of these one would say the ones which are least likely to imply opinions about history are those which depend upon the divisions of time, the simple statements that the common characteristic which unites certain people or certain events is that they lived or took place within the same ten, or fifty or hundred years. It is, however, significant that even into such simple statements there flow the colours and impressions which have been developed from the study of history. As a result the names of the centuries, which are after all only arbitrary groupings of years, take on new and richer meanings from the supposed characteristics of what happened in them. The names of the 19th century, of the 18th century, of the 12th century or of the 5th century B.C. all have acquired meanings which extend far beyond a simple statement about the passage of a hundred years. Even decades sometimes acquire nicknames, though these are often more trivial and journalistic.

This is an interesting example of the way in which opinions about history come to dominate the presentation and understanding of history. It is indeed a necessary process unless the word 'history' is to be confined to the framework of the facts which underlie history. A sense of period is not only an opinion about history, it is needed for the understanding of history. Without a sense of period it would be impossible to grasp the inwardness of many of the events which have taken place, or to interpret the motives of the actors. Without a sense of period it would be difficult for men and women to grasp the critical historical lesson of context, and in order to recognize the processes of history it is desirable to compare the characteristics and ethos of one period with those of another. Yet this sense of period presents the dangers which are always present when men are tempted to mistake opinions for facts. It is easy to slip into the assumption that what are held to be the characteristics of a period are inherent in the facts themselves and are not the result of generalizations by historians. This mistake may have several unfortunate results. It often leads to a curious superficiality of judgement. It is felt that once the period label has been slapped down on something further description and analysis is unnecessary. 'This is all you know on earth, and all you need to know'; least of all will it be necessary to revise the ready made judgement so conveniently supplied. There is nothing about which it is safe to be so easily satisfied. It is therefore important, not only to be able to use insights which the conception of historic periods give, but to be able to criticize them and possibly to escape from them as well. The easiest criticisms suggest themselves when an arbitrary division of time like a century has been taken as having some special significance. It should be sufficiently obvious that round figures count for nothing and that there is not likely to have been a drop of the curtain and a change of scene whenever two noughts entered the date. It is however curiously true that the century number does exercise an unconscious effect on anyone's mind, and it is as well from time to time to purge the results of this tendency by reflecting how utterly without meaning the change from one century to another may be and performing the exercise of redistributing some section of history which one knows well, into significant periods which consciously disregard the conventional division into numbered centuries.

These are relatively easy tasks because of the obvious fallacy of associating significant change with the blind movements of the calendar. It may seem to be more difficult to criticize those divisions into periods which are not based upon this fallacy but upon historical knowledge and historical thought. To do this it is, of course, necessary to test the original concept with wider historical knowledge and profounder historical thought and to see whether these have a dissolvent effect. But as historical scholarship develops this work is always going on, and the extent to which new historical thought and knowledge can revise, and in many ways render meaningless, once universally accepted divisions of history can perhaps be seen in the fate of the old convenient tripartite arrangement of European history into ancient history, medieval history and modern history, which has left deep, apparently permanent, marks on human thought.

This arrangement was originally based on a reasonably clear picture of European history. In the beginning was the ancient world, the world of Greece and Rome with possibly, as a not altogether comfortable addition, the world of the Bible. But religion apart the classical age of Greece and Rome was the age in which civilization originated, and in that age it had also probably reached its highest point. It was followed by a sad period of decline. The ancient world came to an end possibly with the last of the Antonine Emperors, or with the triumph of Christianity, or with the success of the Barbarian invasions,

events loosely connected in many minds. There ensued a prolonged period of 'Gothic' barbarism and superstition, when the
lights of Europe burnt very low. However civilization returned
in the 15th and 16th centuries with the revival of ancient
learning, the 'recovery of letters' as it used to be called, or the
'Renaissance' as it is more normally called nowadays, and at
about that point in time modern history began, as it still does
in the regulations of a good many universities.

At no point has the progress of historical thought and knowledge left this picture undisturbed. Archaeological research has
disclosed infinitely long and important perspectives stretching
back to a much more remote point in time than the Greece that
seemed to be revealed by classical literature. In that long
procession of cultures it would be hard to choose any precise
moment for the beginning of the 'ancient world', or for that
matter to say confidently when or where civilization started.
Nor would it be easy to say when the ancient world came to an
end. It is true that Roman order finally broke down in Western
Europe in the 5th century, but the Empire continued vigorously
in the East and maintained a civilization the importance of
which is only now being realized. The ancient culture was
transmitted to the Arabs who developed it in their own way and
passed it back into Western Europe. But in fact there was
hardly a moment in history when there were not some places,
even in Western Europe, where the old culture was in some way
preserved, though they might be in unexpected places like
Christian Ireland. And there were few periods when it was not
seeping back in one way or another into places where it had
been obscured. There was in fact not one recovery of letters;
there were a great many, if in the dangerous and fluid conditions of this period of the folk wanderings there were always
renewed dangers of loss and destruction.

There was therefore no thousand year 'medieval' interlude
in the development of modern European civilization. It is true
that much that might be called 'barbarism' was brought in by
the nations into the Roman Empire from outside, and much
that might be called 'civilized' perished in the lands where the
Roman order broke down. But even from that 'barbarism' have
been inherited things which were important for the development of Europe as we know it today. Moreover there were

constant, and ultimately successful, attempts at revival and reconstruction, each adding its own contribution to what was coming. There was the Carolingian renaissance and Empire, and there was the great flowering of the human spirit in Western Europe in the 12th century which produced some of the greatest triumphs in art and architecture of which man is capable as well as an important period of political consolidation and a critical development in philosophy. There were, of course, setbacks, and there survived much that we would consider to be 'uncivilized'; as there had been much that was uncivilized in the Roman Empire. But in due course an organized life was developed in Europe which was in fact as significant for the modern world as anything that came in from antiquity at the renaissance, if the renaissance is placed in the 15th and 16th centuries.

Therefore if this old division of European history is looked at from the vantage point of the historical thought of the last hundred years it is clear that the name 'Ancient' is equivocal, the phrase 'Middle Ages' is meaningless—it is used now simply as a convenient label for part of the period it used to cover—and the word 'modern', when not used as a slang word by tradesmen who wish to commend their goods or young people their way of life, could be used for a period which might be held to start with the beginnings of Ionian philosophy, or with the splitting of the atom, or anywhere else in between.

Yet though historical thought has pulverized the old periods of history it has replaced them with other periods and divisions. It is easier now to see unities in other, usually much shorter, stretches of the past and a great deal of what is most significant in the analysis of history has been devoted to describing these unities and the different stages of European development. This type of revision is indeed one way in which historical knowledge develops, and brings those who use it nearer to a correct apprehension of reality. The old generalizations, the old generic statements, give place to new ones which yield new insights, the old categories are replaced by improved categories, which give a more adequate account of whatever it is they contain.

But the patterns of history, the generic statements and categories which we have learnt to use, may have to suffer a more drastic form of criticism. It may be suggested that there are no patterns at all, or, a more likely suggestion, that discernible patterns are superficial and may be deceptive, since, if you look at it closely, each individual case has so much that is idiosyncratic about it, so much that is not explicable in the terms of any category in which it may be cast, that it may be most realistic to forget about categories and present each case separately.

For instance it would seem to be clear that what is important about Shakespeare is not that he was a man of the late 16th and early 17th centuries, or of the Renaissance, or an 'Elizabethan' whatever that may mean, but that he was Shakespeare, and that to consider him under any other title would be to misunderstand his nature and to miss his greatness. Of course the unique quality of Shakespeare is peculiarly obvious because of his supreme genius, but it may be claimed that there is something unique in every individual case that may be cited; that in every human being, every event, every work of art, there is something which cannot be explained in the terms of any category in which it might be placed. It is possible that the word 'unique' is unacceptable, since it implies philosophical possibilities which not everyone would allow. Even so the proposition could be put in this way. All human beings, events or works of art can be grouped into more than one category and to concentrate on the fact that they belong to any one category in particular may easily obscure the significance of the fact that they belong to others as well. To concentrate on a man's period might obscure the influence of his economic position; to describe him solely in terms of his economic position and his century might leave out of account the influence of the part of the country that he comes from. Even to take all these things into consideration may still be to neglect the importance of the psychological type in which he should be classed. But to argue in this fashion will reach the same practical result as would the simple statement that as a human being he was unique, particularly as it is almost certain that not enough will be known about his psychology to classify him accurately. At any rate he is not likely to be adequately explained solely by reference to any of the simple categories historians are likely to use.

It will be convenient, with a slight misuse of terms, to call this tendency *nominalism* after the medieval philosophical school, which claimed that 'universals' or abstract categories were mere names and not realities at all. It is in moderation an healthy tendency. Some historians, particularly those young historians who have only recently got beyond the conception that history is no more than a simple narrative, are often tempted to see history as a kind of game of dominoes played with historical generalizations and abstractions. To counter this tendency it is as well to be reminded that any historical label or abstraction is nothing more than a generalization made by historians to cover a large number of individual cases, that each of these cases have other characteristics than those to which the abstraction refers. Anything which reminds students of this has a useful antiseptic tendency. Perhaps for this reason the study of biography might play a larger part in the normal historical syllabus than it does, for biography concentrates on the human being in the round and not on the categories into which general history is often sorted.

Yet though modified nominalism is an healthy dissolvent, pure or absolute nominalism is an impossibility. Historical categories or abstractions are not illusions, they are necessary for the understanding of history. Without them the reader of history would be so much further from reality. Much old-fashioned Shakespearian criticism and commentary did in fact make this mistake. The commentators failed to make allowance for the influence upon Shakespeare's work of the values of the period in which it was written. They tried to see the plays in the terms of eternal values, which were for them the values of their own time. As a result they left out of account factors in Shakespeare's thought and approach to life which were natural to Shakespeare's age, but foreign to that of A. C. Bradley.

There is, of course, no real contradiction here. Shakespeare was both himself, and a man of the late 16th and early 17th century. Shakespearean criticism can take one of two lines. It can investigate with increasing subtlety and knowledge the significance for Shakespeare of the age in which he lived; or it can try to study Shakespeare as an unique individual, not be wholly explained by reference to any generalizations men have made about his epoch. Either approach may yield new knowledge and new insights; either approach developed alone is liable to cause misconceptions. The same two modes of criticism can be applied to other periods and other people. In the past, even sometimes today, writers were prepared to apply to all the people who flourished between 1837 and 1901 the common adjective 'Victorian'. Recently more and more people have come to reflect that that period is, in modern terms, a long one and that Britain was in that period a complex community which was changing very rapidly, and so they have divided the period up at least into 'late', 'middle' and 'early' Victorian and have marked the great differences in the habits and ways of thought of different sections of the population in each of the different periods. All this revision has no doubt added to the better understanding of those human beings who lived at that time, but it cannot fully explain any one of them. No one can have been a middle class early Victorian, and nothing more: he will also have been a man and have hidden in his heart the complexities and inscrutabilities common to all men. Even if it is impossible to learn much about him it will be important to remember the difference between the human being and the label, for it is important to remember the difference between the facts upon which history is based and the concepts which men have created to explain history.

It is important to remember this in relation to other generic statements than those which primarily refer to the problem of period. Clearly there are other groups which share a common factor, which is different from mere co-existence at the same time, but which may survive through many periods and be in some way independent of them.

Take the various styles in architecture—such as romanesque, gothic, renaissance, baroque. Each of these is firmly rooted in a particular period. It was developed in that period, it can only be studied through it. The general historical criticism which can throw light on that period will throw light on the artistic patterns it developed, while the contemplation of individual examples of each style may teach something which no generalization can teach. But the style itself can survive the period that produced it. It can linger on into later ages of which it is in no way typical. It can be reproduced in an age which is separated by centuries from the era in which it first appeared.

It is something which has appeared in history, and to the understanding of which a sense of period probably should contribute, but which involves something which is in its way independent of history.

There are clearly a good many generic statements of general use in history writing which share this characteristic. Sometimes what is independent of history is an idea, a creed like Christianity or Mohamedanism; sometimes it is an institution that survives through the ages like a Church or a nation; sometimes it is an economic habit that recurs as common economic patterns reproduce themselves. However if it is something which presents a common characteristic in a number of human beings it may be more difficult to discuss what is permanent in it than it is to discuss the nature of an architectural or artistic style. A style can be studied as it still appears in durable buildings and works of art which, with luck, will last from one generation to another, but a creed, an economic habit and in many cases an idea can only be studied through the medium of statements about the actions or thoughts of human beings, who are by no means durable and who cannot hope to last beyond the natural term of years of their generation.

There are, indeed, various reasons why satisfactory generic statements about human beings are peculiarly difficult to make. One of the reasons for this has already been suggested. A man or woman is more complex than any dead object and contains more unknown potentialities. It is always possible that some factor in his make-up may make nonsense of any category in which he is likely to be placed. There may have been some quirk of character that made him accept a creed in a way that could not be expected, or he might have had some unexpected interest that might make nonsense of the pattern of behaviour which his economic position made probable. Sometimes what may make him eccentric may be hidden in his personality, but sometimes it may be a factor of which account might be taken if it were known. But it may not be known. Indeed even if he is alive, or only recently dead, very little, if anything may be known about him, and such knowledge as may be wanted to explain him is even less likely to be available if he belonged to an earlier century with sparser records. Perhaps one of the most useful lessons which any honest attempt to do social research will usually teach is how little can ever be known about how many people, and how difficult it is to make general statements about them with any certainty that they have much relation to reality, particularly when they are statements about feelings and opinion. For these are apt to escape any record that can be reduced to statistics.

Clearly, however, these difficulties do not trouble a great many writers, both journalists and historians. The work of both seems often enough to be riddled with very confident general statements, either made directly or implied by the use of an abstraction which involves a generalization. 'The bulk of the nation was horrified at the callous slaughter of their fellow-citizens in St Peter's Fields Manchester'. 'The upper classes welcomed the doctrine of Malthus since it relieved them from a sense of responsibility for the suffering round them'. 'In the 1930's the tax-paying classes resented the payment of the dole to men who were not supporting themselves by their own labour'. 'The Victorian pater familias' or 'the early Victorian lady' or 'the mid-Victorian working man' 'thought' this, 'felt' that, 'expected' the other thing. It is as well to note statements such as these in one's casual historical reading, and then to go through the exercise of asking oneself two questions. How could the writers know what truth there was in what they were saying, and how can we know upon what evidence their assertions were based?

The problem of the evidence which can be used to support generic statements is a difficult one. I intend to use the next chapter to discuss it, and it will have to be confessed that many such statements can only be based on the impressions of the writer or perhaps on the impressions of contemporary observers. Possibly such evidence can never be decisive; it can however be valuable. To be of any value, however, an impression must have been formed after a reasonably comprehensive review of its subject matter, and it is impossible to believe that before many of these assertions were made any such review had taken place. Often enough the group about which the statement is made is too extensive or too ill-defined for any review of its characteristics to have been possible, or the statement purports to describe the state of mind of very large numbers of people about which there can be no evidence to review. In fact it seems clear enough that in very many cases these statements are casually thrown out by writers who have given no thought at all to the difficult problem of the possible relationship of such a general statement and anything that could be called reality.

They are simply facile guesses, or the scarcely veiled expression of their authors' preconceptions and prejudices. Even so they may exercise considerable power for they often embody in a peculiarly convincing form strong human passions. When they are historical statements they are most dangerous when they claim to describe identifiable groups which have both played their part in history and are still important in current human affairs. The most obvious examples of such groups are nations, such as the French nation, or Churches, such as the Roman Catholic Church; but they include any other body or group which has had a continuous institutional or ideological existence lasting for several centuries. To such bodies permanent characteristics are attributed, they receive praise or blame for the actions for which they have been responsible in the past as if they were men and women, and often indeed they excite the same feelings of love and, more often, of hatred as do men and women.

In fact it will be useful to consider such groups as *collective or historical personalities*. As such the parts they play in history are likely to be more continuous and more relevant to the present day than the actions of the real men and women who appear on the stage for no more than their allotted moment and statements about their characteristics and past actions are likely to excite more lasting and more dangerous emotions in men and women primarily concerned with their own contemporary situation than statements about any ordinary mortal human being, however eminent or disastrous. After he dies an ordinary human being may, it is true, be remembered for a time with love or hatred, but those feelings will fade unless he has become the symbol of something which remains alive after his death, as for instance of one side of one of those perennial controversies, like the quarrels between nations, which divide mankind. A Church or a nation will remain part of the contemporary scene. The good or evil that it did yesterday, it may be preparing to do tomorrow. Therefore its historical character is likely to seem to be of contemporary relevance to each successive generation. For this reason it is peculiarly necessary that generic statements about collective historical personalities should be considered very carefully.

Three types of historical personality are specially important as being, potentially, the focal points of strong passions. They are *nations*, *races* and *classes*. In an earlier age it would have been necessary to add Churches, or historic religions; but the storm centres have for the moment moved elsewhere. It is just possible that in modern circumstances it would be desirable to add an organized ideology like *Communism* which now has a record and has evinced characteristics of its own in history, in fact has become in many ways an historic personality, but it is not clear how long this will enjoy an autonomous existence. It may be objected that a *class* may not be an historic personality in the same way that a nation is likely to be. For a nation is likely to survive as an organic unit for a long period of human history, but a class is likely to disappear after a relatively short time, or to be fundamentally changed, as the result of inevitable changes in the social or economic system which brought it into existence. It is likely however to survive by analogy. If a particular aristocracy or a particular middle class has passed into limbo there is likely to be in existence another aristocracy and another middle class to whom will be credited the qualities and tendencies which that history seems to reveal that aristocracies and middle classes have always possessed. For this reason it is probably as important to scrutinize statements about social classes quite as carefully as statements about nations and races.

If *nations* are sovereign states the problem of considering statements about them may seem deceptively easy. For one thing they present no problem of definition. France, the United Kingdom, the United States, Germany are entities in international law. There can be no question about their nature, or about what they include. As legal entities they can take action as if they were ordinary personalities, and their actions will take effect; the force of them will be recognized by other nations, and they may be held responsible for them. None of this raises any difficulty. The statement that Great Britain declared war on Germany in both 1914 and 1939 presents no problems; the problems begin when the statement is changed to the statement that Great Britain was willing to fight Germany in 1914 and 1939. Probably in each case this statement is substantially true. In 1914 after the invasion of Belgium, and in 1939 after the final rape of Czecho-Slovakia and the attack on Poland, most people in Britain were convinced that they would have to fight Germany. But this attribution of a state of mind to a country can only be substantially true. Both in 1914 and in 1939 there were in Britain people who did not think it right to fight at all. In 1914 there were also those who did not see any need or duty to fight on that occasion, in 1939 there were those who had been instructed to believe that this was an 'imperialist' war from which they should hold aloof. On each occasion there were probably others who were bewildered, who did not understand what had come upon them, but who were prepared to endorse, rather blindly, the action which their government had taken on their behalf.

If this analysis is correct the sum does not add up to the simple statement that Great Britain, as a body of men and women, 'were willing' to fight the Germans in either 1914 or 1939. Probably this does not matter; the substantial truth is what matters and was in each case sufficient. Much more important, and problematical, is the truth or otherwise of a proposition which reverses and extends the original statement, the proposition that 'Germany desired war in 1914 and in 1939'. If this is true it may be of the utmost significance. For in either case the feeling of the British was clearly their reaction to a situation which they had not themselves brought about. If they had sinned, theirs were sins of omission. On the other hand a German will to war may have been one of the factors which created that situation, and, without wishing to pass moral judgements or to suggest legal responsibilities, we must hold that it is crucially important for mankind to diagnose what factors cause wars. But how far is such a statement true for 1914 or in 1939, and if in either case it was true in what way was it true? How many Germans positively wished for war on either occasion? If they existed who were they, and why did they want it? With how many was it a settled opinion, and how many were caught up in a moment of thoughtless national excitement? How many were simply bewildered? How many in

either case viewed the prospect of war with little more than
sickening fears for their country, or for their sons and husbands?
How many actually disapproved of what their country was
doing?

These are important questions. It is important for the
ordinary reader of history to realize that, if he asked them, it
would be difficult for him to gain clear answers to any of them.
Possibly no clear answers are possible. There is a large literature on the causes of the war of 1914–18 and on the crisis
that occupied the last few weeks of peace. It tends, however,
to be more concerned with the opinions of monarchs, statesmen
and soldiers than with what ordinary people felt. There is a
certain amount of evidence about popular feeling in Germany.
Before the war there had been much nationalist talk. There
was a good deal of noisy enthusiasm when the war broke out,
and the opposition of the social democrats proved to be un-
expectedly feeble. When the war seemed to have gone well
some rather surprising people seem to have been anxious to
consolidate and retain possession of the conquests that had been
made. But whether all this adds up to a determined will to war
on the part of the German nation, whether if the rulers of
Germany had themselves been more peaceful in intention, or,
in June and July 1914, more determined to direct affairs
towards a peaceful solution, the bellicose feeling of part of the
German nation would have been coherent enough and effective
enough to have played any part in international affairs are
questions which only an expert can discuss—and perhaps no
one can answer.

The problem of 1939 is even more difficult because of the
tight grip of Hitler's régime on all expressions of German
opinion. Indeed the question seems largely to narrow down to
the relationship of the Nazis to German opinion in general, a
relationship which probably changed between the last free
general election before Hitler came into power and the moment
when the Nazis had been in power for some time and had
begun to shew sensational successes. Even so it is clear that at
any moment there were those in the army who did not want
war. There were also very courageous pacifist groups in
Germany who paid the penalty for their opinions, and the
enthusiasm with which Neville Chamberlain was received in

Germany in 1938 seems to suggest that there were a good many ordinary people in Germany who were anxious for peace.

It seems difficult to fuse all these facts into the simple statement that the German nation desired war in either 1914 or in 1939, or indeed that the 'German nation' at any times, as a nation, 'wanted' anything. Whatever the truth may have been it was an extremely complicated truth and it requires elaborate and delicate research to reveal it; and in all probability parts of it never can be revealed. The same is true of any statement that ascribes a common intention to any very large body of men and women.

Yet such statements, unqualified and unquestioned, fill the pages of history books, particularly of elementary history books. For instance those who read examination papers know that there is a general impression, at least among the young who are learning history, that in the middle of the 19th century an overwhelming factor in the formation of French opinion was a passionate desire for military glory, which the writers normally call 'la gloire' to shew that they know what they are about. But what is the truth of this? How many Frenchmen, and how many Frenchwomen, really wished to return to the splendours and miseries of the time of Napoleon I? There was at various times in the 19th century a good deal of noisy journalism and no doubt much military boasting and café talk, but the confidential reports of the state of public opinion which the government of the second Empire always received as a matter of routine from its procureurs généraux and its prefects seem to reveal that large sections of public opinion were by no means inebriated in this way and were inclined not to want war, or, when as in 1859 they had permitted themselves to be involved in war, were anxious to get out of it.[1]

The statements which ascribe positive warlike intentions to the Germany of William II or of Adolf Hitler or to the France of Napoleon III are not therefore in any simple sense true. But there is truth in them and it is truth of considerable historical importance. There was enough noisy imperialism in the France of the Second Empire to lead France into the folly and disaster of 1870. And not only was there enough

[1] Lynn M. Case, *French opinion on War and Diplomacy during the Second Empire* (Philadelphia, 1954).

determination in Germany in both 1914 and 1939 to steel the
Germans to put up a tremendous fight which hardly faltered
until ultimate defeat, but both before 1914 and 1939 the virus
of aggressive nationalism seems to have deeply infected the
German spirit. It seems to have been latent in statesmen in
whom its presence was not suspected and it also produced the
situation which made Nazism and the Nazi control of Germany
possible. It is as difficult with all these facts in mind to deny,
as it was to accept, the proposition that there was in Germany
a will to war, which was an important factor in the history of
humanity at two very critical moments.

It is of course easy to resolve the paradox by saying that
some Germans wanted war and others did not, but this,
obviously true, commonplace does not seem to contain the
whole truth; nor to be frank the most important part of the
truth. What is at issue is not just what men and women happened to think at a particular moment if they thought at all,
but whether there was in Germany what might be called a
general tendency of feeling which made it probable that
opinion, even among the undecided and uncommitted, would
crystallize in a certain direction, and that certain creeds and
attitudes could develop which could not have developed in
other countries, so that actions and policies were likely to be
approved in Germany which might not have been acceptable
elsewhere. This however raises a further question. If such
tendencies as these exist in a country when have they developed?
Are they likely to be the product of very recent conditions?
Or could they have been developed over a much longer period
of a country's history? Could they indeed have their roots in
very remote times?

Such questions propose a new problem about nations and
nationality. It is clear that in law as a sovereign body, or at
least as an accepted entity, a nation can have an existence
which persists through many centuries, but is it so like a real
human being that it can retain in some way mental habits and
characteristics over long periods? Does each generation inherit
an imponderable legacy from the past which in some way
influences the way in which the minds of the men and women
of a particular nation are likely to work?

At first sight it would have seemed that the probabilities

were against such an inheritance being possible, particularly from before 1800. Times change and men change with them. The whole physical and psychological background to life has changed since 1800 so radically that it would seem clear that, at least in many matters, the men and women of all civilized nations nowadays resemble each other more closely than any of them resemble their own ancestors. More than this, every nation has changed drastically within itself. There is the consistent erosion of habits of thought and custom which is caused by one generation taking the place of another. The history of any nation that has stepped into the modern world will reveal that its social structure has changed, its moral and religious background has changed, its political organization has changed from what they were even a century ago. Is it therefore to be believed that through all these changes something has survived which inclines men to think in some ways as their compatriots thought two or three hundred years since? It may be reasonable to hope that 'there will always be an England' but that there always has been an England, or that for any appreciable length of time there has been an England which is anything like the England we know, seems to be a much more dubious proposition.

Yet speaking cautiously and keeping in mind all the reservations and exceptions which must be made when propounding any generalization about a large number of people, it does seem that there are such things as reasonably permanent national characteristics. Such characteristics are closely associated with a nation's institutions, but they operate in a sphere beyond the reach of institutions and can remain the same if a nation's institutions have been revolutionized. They are fed by a nation's culture, but they are effective among those whom that culture hardly reaches. They change as elements enter or leave the life of a nation, yet the changes are those of organic growth uniting what is new with what is continuous, not the replacement of one thing by something which is different. They seem to be realities and if realities they are important.[1]

[1] There is a large literature dealing with the important problem of the nature of National Characteristics. A short and very stimulating essay on the subject is Ernest Renan, *Qu'est-ce qu'une Nation?* (Paris, 1882). An interesting modern view is to be found in J. L. Talmon, *The Unique & the*

Yet their nature is not to be assumed too easily, and it is particularly important to realize that what men of one nation say about themselves is normally what they wish to have believed in their favour, and what they say about the characteristics of their neighbours is quite likely to be their case against them, or at least to be strongly coloured by their own recent or contemporary relations with them. For instance this is the way the great French 19th century historian Michelet described the English when discussing the fate of Joan of Arc. 'This great English people among so many good and solid qualities has one vice which spoils these very qualities. This vast and profound vice is pride', (orgueil) 'cruel malady but one which is none the less the principle of their life, the explanation of their contradictions and the secret of their acts' . . . 'This adoration of self, this inward looking cult of the creature for its own sake, is the sin by which Satan fell, the supreme impiety. This is why with so many human virtues, with their serious and honest appearance, with their touch of the spirit of the bible, no nation is further from grace. This is the only nation which could not make the imitation of Jesus its own; [he had been speaking of the 15th century book *The Imitation of Christ*] a Frenchman could have written that book, a German or an Italian, but never an Englishmen. From Shakespeare to Milton, from Milton to Byron their beautiful and sombre literature is sceptical, judaic, satanic, to sum up anti-christian.' He concludes with these remarkable words. 'Les Indiens de l'Amerique, qui ont tant de pénétration et d'originalité, disaient à leur manière: "Le Christ, c'était un Français que les Anglais crucifièrent à Londres, Ponce-Pilate était un officier au service de la Grande Bretagne".'[1]

It may be the result of English 'orgueil', but to an Englishman some of the details of this description seem overdrawn. It is however only fair to remember that when Michelet was

Universal (1965), particularly in the first article, pp. 11–63. The footnotes to this article give a useful guide to further reading on the subject. I discussed the history of the English national tradition in my book *The English Inheritance* (1950) and said something on what I thought were the English national characteristics.

[1] J. Michelet, *Histoire de France au moyen age: Jeanne D'Arc* (Paris, 1898), pp. 269–70.

writing quite as absurd things were being written about the
French in England; about their levity, their vanity, their
Revolutionary propensities—'the red fool-fury of the Seine',
their tendency to sexual extravagances and their lack of
domestic virtues—it was said with gloomy satisfaction that
'there was no word 1or *home* in the French language'. But of
course the nonsense produced on either side of the Channel was
begotten by hostility out of ignorance. It was largely the result
of the long struggle between Britain and France, which may
have culminated at Waterloo but which reverberated for the
rest of the century.

In the 20th century the diplomatic pattern of Europe changed
and with it men's views of the permanent characteristics of the
nations who were their neighbours. In Britain, France was
viewed much more favourably; it was the nature of Germany
which was now subjected to severe diagnosis. An extreme
example can be found in Lord Vansittart's pamphlet *Black
Record* published during the last war. In it Germany was
described as the 'butcher bird' of Europe always ready to
pounce and tear and slaughter. 'This bird of prey', he said, 'is
no sudden apparition. It is a species. Hitler is no accident. He
is the natural and continuous product of a breed, which since
the dawn of history has been predatory and bellicose'.[1]

Yet there is something here which must give pause. Between
1933 and 1939 Vansittart was at the Foreign Office in Britain
and, partly because of his view of the German nation, he saw
more clearly than most Britons, certainly than his immediate
political masters, the danger that was building up in Germany.
It is the old dilemma. It is impossible to accept without serious
reservations the things which are said about the intentions and
the characteristics of nations, but it is also impossible to reject
these things absolutely without incurring the danger of shutting
one's eyes to realities which may be of the most urgent importance.

It is also possible that hatred, like love, may reveal things
which indifference is unable to see. This was true of Lord
Vansittart; and perhaps, then, there was some basic truth
behind Michelet's description of English 'orgueil'. But the

[1] Sir Robert Vansittart, *Black Record: Germans Past and Present* (1941),
p. 16.

matter cannot satisfactorily be left to revelations inspired by love or hatred. If there is anything in these matters, and, if what there is is important, it is necessary that it should not be left to be no more than the subject matter of angry assertion in moments of international tension; it should rather be subjected to careful historical analysis in moments of relative indifference. For instance there are certain questions which might be asked *now*, when the pressure is off, about the nature of Nazism. To what extent was it something which has analogies in the 20th century elsewhere than in Germany? To what extent was it something which 20th century conditions might favour in any country, a violent demagogical creed seasoned with pseudo-science and appealing to the brutal but generous enthusiasms of a youth which has repudiated the old ethical sanctions? Or to what extent was it something essentially German, receiving its force from the frustrations of Germany's peculiar position after the defeat in 1918, and which could not have developed in any other cultural tradition than the German? Probably it is impossible to give an assured answer to these questions, but it seems probable that much more could be learnt about them if they were asked now.

The conception of *race* is often closely associated with the ideas behind nationalism, though it is possible to have a conception of nationalism which does not depend upon a conception of race, if by a *race* is meant a group of people who, because they share a common descent and a common blood relationship, have inherited certain common moral and intellectual characteristics. The conception of race is, nowadays, reasonably viewed with deep suspicion since it was the basis of the detestable doctrine and practice of the Nazis, and emerges in the troublesome prejudices which develop when two races of different colours inhabit the same district. However in the 19th century a very various, and in some cases highly respectable, body of thought accepted the doctrine of race without question. It was used by a romantic like Disraeli, and, as it sometimes still is, by a number of literary and artistic critics to explain this or that quality in the writers or painters whom they were discussing. Reasonably serious historians talked wisely about such things as the inherent characteristics of the 'Norman', the 'Saxon' and the 'Celt'. But what is more important is that it was readily accepted by leading scientists, and elaborate theories were built upon the measurements of skulls, the colours of eyes and hair, the shapes of noses, as also on the evidence of philology. Using these tests humanity was divided up into a number of dominant types each with its own peculiar moral and mental characteristics.[1]

The names of races are often used today and particular characteristics are often attributed to them, but of this elaborate scientific superstructure nothing remains. The literature about it stands as a permanent memorial to the extent and variety of the conclusions which intelligent men can base on doubtful or irrelevant evidence. It is of course observably true that among various groups of people who inhabit the same area the same physical characteristics often predominate. They have, for instance, fair hair, blue eyes, straight noses, and so on. Whether this means they have the kind of racial history racialists would claim for them is uncertain; probably not if it is claimed that they are of 'pure' or 'unmixed' stock, whatever that may mean. But whatever the truth about some common factor which may be called 'race', it would be exceedingly difficult to assert with any confidence that any common mental or moral characteristics they may shew are attributable to their common physical characteristics. A group, which shares such common physical characteristics, is also likely to have had a common history, to share a common cultural inheritance, to have faced common economic necessities, to be organized in a common social structure and be the subject of the same politics. In order to assert that any common mental and spiritual characteristics, which such a group may seem to share, derive, not from one of these common influences, but from a common physical inheritance which is the embodiment of 'race', is to set aside what is obvious, identifiable and intelligible in favour of a factor which if it exists is hard to isolate, difficult to define and the effects of which must, as far as knowledge goes at the moment, rest entirely on supposition.

If it were demonstrably true that men and women of a

[1] See Jacques Barzun, *Race: A Study in Superstition Revised with a new preface 'Racism Today'*, New York (1965).

particular racial stock always exhibited the same common peculiarities in strongly contrasted social conditions this difficulty might be overcome. It is indeed often asserted that this is so, but the examples given are normally too loosely stated to be taken seriously. Moreover, though the circumstances of their lives may be different, members of a recognizable group are still likely to have other things in common besides their 'racial' inheritance. They are likely to have a common moral and cultural tradition, and they may well have normally found themselves in the same kind of positions as emigrants, officials, settlers or shopkeepers in the lands into which they have travelled. For instance if it were said, as indeed it is often said, that Jews have always developed the same characteristics in any community in which they have lived, it would first have to be asked whether this was demonstrably true; and secondly, if it was true, whether the strong cultural and religious tradition which orthodox Jews carry with them, and the unfortunate position of perpetual alien, and often of despised and persecuted alien, which in many countries they have been forced to occupy, do not amply explain any common Jewish characteristics without resorting to any mysticism about the influence of Jewish blood.

Unfortunately the matter cannot end here. Theories about race were, to an extent that it is difficult now to realize, intellectually respectable in the 19th century and seemed to be endorsed by Darwinism, even if it was largely misunderstood Darwinism. But the force behind such theories was not normally, not primarily, intellectual; it was more often elemental, instinctive and, in the last resort, irrational. Such theories often flourished in what might be called frontier conditions, where people of one culture and nationality confronted the people of another in close contact, particularly perhaps where one nationality wished to retain superiorities which the other challenged. It was not for nothing that much of Hitler's youth was passed in Vienna which is essentially a frontier city, lying as near as it does to the frontier between the German speaking nations and the Slavs, and it is significant that other Nazi leaders came from German communities on the Baltic which were in much the same position. The position in South Africa and in the Southern States of the United States needs no comment.

An analogous situation can develop when a reasonably advanced highly populated community receives a mass immigration from another country with lower economic standards and possibly rather more primitive habits. The flood of immigrants in the 19th century into the U.S.A. from Ireland, South and Eastern Europe, the immigration of the Irish into Britain after 1846, of the Jews into Britain after 1880, or of the Africans, Indians and Pakistani into Britain nowadays are all cases in point. In all of them the same phenomena have appeared. The new immigrants' advent has been resented by those who had to be their neighbours, whether or no the immigrants have seriously competed with the older inhabitants for jobs or living space. Accusations have been brought against them which bear strong family resemblance to accusations brought against other groups of immigrants. It has been said that they have brought disease with them, that the crowded conditions in which they are forced to live reduce standards all round, that they undercut native labour. As a result a greatly enhanced consciousness of race has developed and a soil has been prepared in which dangerous political attitudes and possibly racial theories can grow like poisonous weeds.

It is therefore not possible simply to dismiss the conception of race as something which is too confused and unsubstantial to be taken seriously. It has been the precipitant of strong human emotions, and to understand the motive forces of history it is necessary to consider what men have meant by race, even if what they said was absurd. The things that men say and think as fiercely as they have spoken and thought about race always matter. The divisions of mankind which the historian has to consider are not only those which evident fact or accurate sociological analysis reveal as realities. They must also consider those groups into which men think they are divided, even if it is impossible to find a satisfactory objective principle behind the division.

It is important to remember this also when discussing the category which plays as great a part in much modern historical writing, as the conception of race performed in some 19th century historical work, the category of *the economic or social class*. Often enough a class within a society is presented as a clear-cut economic division of the society, whose interests and behaviour are clearly predetermined by its economic situation. Actually the economic and social position may be complicated and confused. The lines of class may be determined as much by contemporary opinion as by anything else, and what may be conceived to be the economic interests of any particular group may be the result of a contemporary opinion which does not coincide with what more modern analysis suggests it ought to have been.

By *class* should probably be meant any reasonably large section of a community which is united either by a common social status, or by a common economic position, or by both. As a conception it necessarily enters into any account of the structure of any society, and the part played by economic interest in the relationships within the society are likely to be defined in terms of class and the pressure of one class on another. There are, it is true, exceptions to this. A particular individual's pursuit of his own economic interest might be rightly considered to have nothing to do with any particular class. Moreover since the conception of the division of a community into classes usually carries with it something of the idea of the horizontal stratification of society it might be wrong to consider that a number of individuals, who came from different levels in that stratification but had the same economic interest, say were all engaged in the same industry or were all alike investors in the same range of concerns, were members of the same class. Such exceptions may be worth considering, but clearly it is normal for those who are joined by a common economic interest to enjoy the same position in the social hierarchy, and it may be taken that this condition is a necessary component of the conception of a class.

The conception is of considerable importance. It can be used to sum up the common economic interest of large numbers of people, and their economic condition. It helps to express the social structure of a country, which often does not exactly correspond with its economic structure. It is also of great psychological importance. Some of the most dynamic forces in history spring from the feeling of class solidarity and the sense of class conflict.

It is, however, a conception to be used with caution. The problems of definition and delimitation which it presents are often difficult. It is by no means always clear into what class a particular individual should be placed at a particular moment. It is also by no means always clear what at any given moment are the significant classes of a community, particularly in the eyes of the community at the date in question. For instance Britain in the 19th century is apt to be divided into the traditional tripartite division of the upper or aristocratic class, the middle class and the working class; but any reasonably careful observation of British society at any point in that century will disclose a much more complicated and elaborate stratification. This is peculiarly true of the bracket which is supposedly covered by the label 'middle class'.

The middle class is presumably that section of society which lies between the landed gentry and nobility on the one hand and the operatives, the people who labour with their hands, on the other. If so it must range, in 19th century Britain, from city magnates, manufacturers and contractors, who rank with, or compete with, the highest in the land, through a large variety of social groups, each commanding its own standard of life, down to humble shopkeepers and clerks, who found it difficult to maintain with any security any standard at all. At any point in that century every cultural standard was represented in this great mass from some of the most highly educated men and women in the country to people who had just enough literacy to make out a simple bill, or to copy a letter without necessarily understanding its contents. Within their number could be found every political attitude that could be found in the country, every religious denomination and every way of life, from the overwhelmingly respectable to the outrageously disreputable. Indeed so great is the variety of groups in this bracket that if anyone writes or spoke of the British Middle Class in any period in the 19th century it is always permissible, and normally desirable, to put the question: 'Which Middle Class?'

The middle class of 19th century Britain was no doubt more complex than such classes in the smaller pre-industrial societies which had existed in Britain, and elsewhere, in the 18th century and which still survived in various parts of Europe into the 19th century. But the study of pre-revolutionary France suggests how complicated the structure of an advanced pre-industrial pre-19th century society could be. Nor in the 19th century, or in any other century, were the complications only in the middle of society. If the term middle class, or middle classes, is to be satisfactory, then there must be a clear boundary on either side of the sections which are so named. But that boundary has often been shadowy and uncertain. In 19th century Britain there were landowners, and people occupying land, who might, or who might not, be conceived to be gentlemen. There were rich men who were graduating into gentility. There were men of the professional classes—lawyers, doctors, the clergy, army and naval officers and later such people as architects, civil engineers and civil servants—who might be conceived to be gentlemen by reason of function. All these groups might in some analyses be called middle class, in others not. On the line between the middle class and the working class there were independent craftsmen, between whom and the smaller shopkeepers who were only dealers the social difference was non-existent and the economic difference very little. There were very small land holders, who might have to earn part of their livelihood by working on other men's land. There were at times an aristocracy of highly-skilled, highly-paid labour, whose incomes and interests might unite them rather to the middle classes than to the less skilled, less well-paid, working classes beneath the shadow line.

Above and below these two frontier regions there have normally been other complications. Among the aristocracy there was very often an important division between the large landowners and the great nobility on the one hand and the smaller landowners and gentry on the other. Among the working classes there have normally been endless gradations between those who had a small holding, or were skilled in a trade, and those men and possibly still more often those women, who had literally nothing, not even much that they could call a home. Different economic interests—agricultural, mercantile or manufacturing—often crossed the horizontal lines of class, and in a society like that of Britain in the 19th century which did not have the strictly defined hierarchy of castes which exist in more primitive societies the realities of class as often as not rather had roots in psychology than the results of economic function or condition. A man might be a member of the middle classes mainly because he felt that he belonged to the middle class, or other people felt that he did. A man or a woman might come to identify themselves with the working class partly because their economic position made it natural for them to do so, and partly because there had developed the conception of an entity which could be called 'the working class' with which they could identify themselves.

The problems which the definition and delimitation of social and economic classes present are therefore difficult. They are the more so since the class structure, and what people think about the class structure, changes as society changes and develops. Yet it is very important for the reader of history to be clear in his mind on these questions, for a great deal of history may well be presented to him in terms of class, and it is important for him to be on his guard against fallacies which this method of presentation may assume.

For instance the conditions of life of certain sections of society may be presented in the terms of the standard of life of the class of which they are conceived to be members. But if too large a section of the community is taken as constituting that class, and an average rate of earning is worked out by taking the receipts of all that class together, that average may have little or no relevance to the problems of the group in question whose earnings may all be consistently below, or consistently above, the average which is proposed as in some way representing their condition.

Or it may be assumed that the politics and economic aspirations and enmities of particular groups in the country were orientated in a certain direction because they were on one side or other of the lines which are believed to divide the working class from the middle class, or the middle class from the aristocracy; when in fact one group, though apparently working class, may have felt a strong identity of interest with the middle class, and another group, though apparently middle class, were anxious to graduate into the ranks of the gentry and were determined to pursue the objects and share the prejudices of the class with which they wished to be numbered. But in all cases any assumption that it is easy to deduce what a man's motives were from the economic class, of which it is believed that he was a member, should be viewed with caution. In certain cases, too, the classical theory of class conflict may be misleading. Working men may feel a sense of solidarity with their employers, or tenants with their landlords, particularly if in either case both groups seem to be threatened by a third group, whose interests are foreign to the interests of both. One group of workers may regard as their most dangerous enemies another group of workers even though they would both appear to be of the same economic class. Therefore in all cases assumptions about what men ought to have felt should be checked by evidence of what they actually did feel before they can be satisfactorily accepted.

Even when a man's mind was wholly concentrated on his own particular economic interest a modern mind may easily be mistaken in its assumptions about what he was likely to think would serve him best. He might for instance have put his faith in a national policy of free trade and free enterprise when we believe he would have been best protected by a policy of state intervention and socialism, or he may have favoured protection where we should have expected him to support a policy of free trade. But it will be his mind which made the calculation not ours, and it is our duty to find out what way his mind worked not to impose our thoughts upon it. When it is a rich man who is in question it may not be clear which of a variety of conflicting interests he may believe to be the most important. When it is a very poor man the problem may be whether he is conscious of more than the immediate needs of the moment. The extent to which a man is conscious of his class will alter as history develops, as will also the way in which he is conscious of it. In addition to this men will look on a class system with different eyes if it is an open class system, in which people easily move from one class to another, or a closed system, in which such movement is difficult, and men cannot look forward to the possibility of promotion to any other class. As conditions change the nature of any class system in this respect will change also.

All these matters must be settled by research into the facts in question not by making *a priori* assumptions. There will also be, **as in all other attempts to sort human beings into categories,** in any individual case the possibilities of what I have called nominalism, the possibility that the idiosyncrasies of the individual may cancel any generalization that might have been made of him as a member of a class. Certainly it is impossible to be sure that a desire to further his economic interests must have provided the dominant motive of any man or woman. Other motives, worthy or unworthy, may have controlled their minds. Religious ardour, or vanity, patriotism or snobbery, pity for other men's sufferings or the meanest or the most malignant personal dislikes and hatreds, all these have affected human beings, and the suggestion that they are 'really' economic motives, or that, if you search long enough and are ingenious enough a dominant economic motive will be found, is likely to lead to sophistry and to tampering with the evidence.

Yet with all these difficulties the conception of social and economic class is a reality, and it is impossible to understand the domestic history of any country without coming to terms with it. It may require more knowledge than is readily available to do this effectively and critically; it probably requires more specialized skill than most people possess, for it is precisely in such matters that the techniques of the sociologist may be useful. But to try to describe a community without reference to class is like trying to describe the anatomy of the human body without reference to its bones. Indeed each of the three forms of collective personality represent in one way important realities, both real divisions of humanity, and ideas in which the springs of action have been hidden. But each as they are often presented in history books provide some very difficult critical problems.

The simple treatment of nations as composite personalities which can think things, will things, feel things is clearly at odds with reality; while what has been said about national characteristics has often been quite equal in nonsense to what has normally been said about race. People who talk about class have very often not done that careful social analysis and research which must be done if discussions about class are to be realistic. They have rather imposed on the subject matter a pre-conceived pattern, which may fit it very badly indeed.

What then is the ordinary reader to do?

His situation is difficult, but there seem to be two or three points which he can observe with advantage.

First he can refuse to tolerate dangerous absurdities. Since the idea of race is often the natural and instinctive reaction to circumstances which are likely to recur, it is very probable that the conception of race, which is discredited at the moment, may reappear in some form, particularly in the kind of popular writing that lies on the borders of history. If it does so any critical reader of history should be able to probe it, realizing that any scientific authority it may claim will be negligible. Nevertheless he should also realize that it will be important to learn what were the circumstances which led to its growth.

Secondly it will be necessary to remember the difficulty of making any general statement about any group, especially any large group, which will be completely true, and how artificial and potentially misleading are many of the statements which are conventionally acceptable, particularly those often made about the common intentions and the characteristics of whole nations. This is an important subject which does not seem to have the scholarly attention which it deserves, on which the ordinary reader of history could with advantage spend a good deal of thought.

However, to make a third point, where there does already exist accurate thought which could correct and perhaps deepen any particular type of generic statement which is often used, it is clearly desirable to become familiar with it. This is true in relation to statements about class. An increasing body of relevant thought is being applied to the analysis of the structure of society and the forces at work in it. It may not be used as much as it ought to be. Many historians are still inclined to fight shy of anything that calls itself sociology. They have some reason for their fears, for that word has sometimes covered the use of over-simplified generalizations perfunctorily based on what is really inadequate evidence to endorse a rather crass and superficial form of determinism. The cure for bad sociology is, however, not to eschew sociology but to use better sociology, and there seems to be little doubt that if in the future any one is going to want to use or to criticize general statements about the groups or classes in society it will be to the work of the sociologists he will, increasingly, have to turn.[1]

If however anyone is going to think clearly about the behaviour and nature of groups that are, at least partly, economic in origin he will have to understand the purely economic structure of society and the economic forces at work in society. To understand these things it is desirable to gain a working knowledge of the ideas economists use and the meaning of their language, and with their help to study how society has been organized and economic forces have affected it in the past. Since this knowledge is fundamental and will affect the content of a good many generalizations in daily use it should probably be acquired at an early stage in a student's educational career. Unfortunately pure economic history has not always been sufficiently studied in schools, and when it has been studied it seems too often to have been studied descriptively rather than analytically. Children have been taught what happened without sufficient attention being paid to the more interesting problems why it happened, or how it happened. At least a number of them seem to have got used to the use of the terms of economic analysis without any very clear idea what they meant, and to the description of economic institutions without much idea what function they have performed. For instance I once came across a number of schoolboys who were prepared to deplore the results of 'Capitalism' and to dilate at some length on the supposed relationship between 'Capitalism' and 'puritanism'. but when asked what 'Capitalism' was could give no coherent answer. And on another occasion, there was a group of candidates for an examination taken at school who had apparently been asked what were the provisions of the Bank Charter Act of 1844 and seem to have given in the main correct answers, at least most of them had done so; but none of them seemed to have any clear idea what functions bankers performed, or what difficulties the act was supposed to control.

The teaching which permitted such things must have made economic history duller than it ought to be and can not have supplied a satisfactory foundation for accurate thought about

[1] T. B. Bottomore, *Classes in Modern Society* (1965), can be recommended as an introduction to the sociological study of class. It contains a useful selected bibliography.

the classes of society. How far it would prevail now I would not know, but even among adults there sometimes seems to be a tendency to ignore the correct use of terms of economic analysis, and to use them, if at all, to express a meaning which they have simply acquired by association. The ways in which the word 'Capitalism' is sometimes used is in fact a case in point.

Such loose thought is unlikely to lead to the satisfactory classification and description of the various groups within society. Its prevalence suggests the value of two questions which the ordinary reader might well ask of any generic statement that is presented to him: What did the author mean by the statement, and was he himself quite clear what he meant? When pressing that enquiry it is peculiarly important to probe all words that look as if they are terms of exact analytical thought, but may have in fact no clearly defined conception behind them.

There is, however, another question which should be asked of any generic statement. It is the obvious one: Upon what evidence does it rest? But to the problem of the evidence which can be used to support such statements I intend to devote the next chapter.

12

The Evidence for Generic Statements—
Myths, Impressions and Quantification

IT IS intrinsically likely that the evidence for generic statements
about groups will provide difficulties not presented by the
evidence about single cases. The evidence which bears on a
particular event or the behaviour of a particular man or woman
may be baffling and inconclusive, but it is at least likely to be
concentrated. It will be ranged round one centre of interest,
and this will help to make the problems it presents easy at the
least to comprehend, if not to solve. But this will probably not
be true of the evidence required to establish some general
statement about a group of one sort or another. Instead of one
central point there will be many, in fact as many as there are
members in the group. The evidence may therefore not be
easy to assemble and to comprehend as a whole, while the
problem of framing a single generic statement which truthfully
expresses common characteristics presented by a large number
of separate individuals may present very considerable intellectual difficulties indeed.

It may also not be easy, or even possible, to recover the
necessary evidence. A group may be important, but its
members obscure. Even if there are records it is quite likely
that they will throw little light on the subject under discussion.
For instance the statements which some historians make with
confidence about the ways of thought of a nation, a class or a
generation are often statements about what went on in the
minds of dead men and women the vast majority of whom,
whatever other record they have left, have left no record of
their opinions but whose thoughts have been inferred from
what would seem to the writer to be the probable attitude of

people in their position, from their supposed assent to actions taken in their name, or from their presumed agreement with statements made by people who seem to have resembled them.

In such circumstances perhaps it may be a mistake to make any general statements about any large group at all, particularly statements about groups of human beings. However if any picture of the past is to be available such general statements have to be made and historians have dealt with these difficulties in one of three ways. They have to a large extent relied on *preconceived ideas*; they have accepted a general theory of history or an historical myth which provides them with an account of the way in which men have thought. They have formed in their minds *a general impression* on the matter, and have allowed their imaginations to supply what might be missing in the evidence, and so have produced a coherent picture. Or, lastly, they have *examined systematically* the details of as many different cases as possible and from the results of this examination have built up their conclusions, possibly using a mathematical calculation to help them to do so.

At first sight it may seem that the third of these methods is the only defensible one. The first process is clearly illegitimate. If a statement is supposed to be historical it must refer to what actually happened in history, not to what is assumed to have happened, and there ought to be some evidence that it has actually happened; and the systematic review of individual facts with the use of mathematical processes to interpret them would seem to be obviously preferable to the impressions which a man may form after a general unsystematized meditation upon the evidence. Apart from the increased accuracy and certainty which the careful enumeration of observed instances affords, system supplies some sort of objective check. Left to itself a man's mind tends to select from what he observes in order to fit it into some acceptable pattern or preconceived idea. By accepting a systematic plan of action, by determining, for instance, to examine all the cases in a particular class, or perhaps a selection of them based on predetermined principles a man has accepted the discipline of something outside himself and beyond the scope of his preferences; while the operations of mathematics should be automatic and independent of the mind of the mathematician.

Nevertheless, though where it is practicable and suitable for the subject the technique of objective systematic research into individual cases, with the use of mathematics to interpret the result, is obviously the best method of arriving at a general truth about a group, it may be doubted whether there is any enquiry which could be tackled by this method alone. Moreover it seems certain that there are some important enquiries in relation to which it would be irrelevant and probably misleading. The intuitive power of the human mind, which works through the power of imagination, or receiving impressions, and not simply through the acceptance of the results of objective calculation plays its part in most, possibly in all general statements; and so, at least in most enquiries, do the patterns, the general theories or myths, which men use to make sense of history and of life.

For in order to organize any enquiry, however systematic and objective it is going to be, a certain number of decisions about its scope and about the nature of its subject matter must be taken by those who are going to conduct it. I will discuss some of the problems which have to be solved later in this chapter; suffice it to say here that they are not problems to which the processes of enumeration and calculation are likely to offer any solution: they rather prescribe the terms on which the processes of enumeration and calculation shall proceed. In doing so whoever is conducting the enquiry must clearly use ideas which existed before the results of the enquiry were known and were not suggested by its results. But the results of the enquiry are likely to be influenced by the way in which these decisions have been taken, particularly so if the results are interpreted in the light of the same ideas as prescribed by the original terms of the enquiry.

It is true that systematic research, and for that matter the insights which unsystematic meditation on the subject may bring, break the pattern which *preconceived ideas* may have imposed; that is indeed one of the ways in which progress in historical knowledge has been achieved. But preconceived ideas are often pretty strong on the wing, they carry a lot of shot. Men require a pattern into which they can fit their discoveries if they are to mean anything, and it is not in human nature for men to be at all ready to change an accepted pattern which appears to make sense of what they are doing. Indeed experience shews what a surprising amount of honest, intelligent, detailed research even a defective pattern can carry before it is realized that it must be put on the shelf.

The pattern which a man is likely to use as a frame for his work is likely to be in part provided by that tangled network of memories, half memories, learning, prejudice and emotional associations which most men carry about with them, and which I tried to describe when I discussed men's individual conceptions of what is probable. But at least part of the pattern of their view of the past may have been provided for them by a theory of history or, what is more likely, an historical myth.

The difference between an historical theory and an historical myth, as I am going to use the term, is this: a theory of history presents a pattern according to which it is conceived things must happen owing to the operation of certain principles; an historical myth presents a pattern according to which it is conceived things have happened. The theory of communism is the theory of the materialist conception of history; the myth of communism is the account of human affairs which it is believed bears out that theory. But myths are not necessarily theories translated into terms of fact. They can have other origins. They may spring from the *ex parte* case for one side to a political or religious controversy which has come to be generally accepted by historians as the whole truth. This may have purported to give an account of events which took place while the controversy was going on, or it may have provided a version of earlier history on which that side based its case. Or an historic myth may be a view of history by virtue of which men of a particular nation feel that their national identity is established. In all these cases an opinion has passed into the record and given it a distinctive shape.

Historical myths are by no means necessarily altogether false. Many of them include important truths and often much can be learned from them, even by those who are not inclined to accept them in their entirety. But they are creations of the human mind and therefore they have always been to some extent imposed on history from outside by men who had a reason for reading a certain pattern into human affairs. They can therefore cause the distortions of facts they use, and also appear to supply certain knowledge which the evidence does not by itself warrant.

A good many examples of important myths could be given. There are of course nationalist, racialist or religious myths. There are myths engendered by the enthusiastic support, or the violent rejection, of the French Revolution or Napoleon. There is the myth of the common people, according to which it is held that the common people have normally been right and virtuous and oppressed by a greedy and conscienceless upper class. But perhaps the myth which comes most easily to hand is the Whig interpretation of English history, with its Liberal extension into the 19th century.

As is so often the case with historical myths this had its origin in a political controversy and represented the case for one side; but so tenacious was its grip on the English mind that when that controversy was really closed it was rather artificially extended to cover other issues and so it became the accepted picture of English history. The controversy in which it originated was the struggle between the Stuart kings and their Parliaments. The opponents of the crown discovered the origins of English freedom and of the English system of Parliamentary government in the institutions and principles of the Saxons before the Norman conquest. After the conquest the rights of Englishmen were endorsed by medieval precedent, particularly by Magna Carta and realized in the history of Parliament. Thus it was claimed that England had had from time immemorial a definite constitution which the Stuart kings were attempting to violate.

That controversy might be said to be closed by the Revolution of 1688 and by the establishment of the House of Hanover on the throne. But on two later occasions it still seemed that the same issues were at stake, and the same forces in collision. At the beginning of George III's reign there was a double controversy which in due course fused into one, first a controversy between George III and various groups of English politicians who were out of office and secondly a controversy between George III and the American colonists. The old pattern was made to cover both these quarrels. It was claimed that inspired by the teaching of Bolingbroke's *Patriot King*, George III had tried to return to the arbitrary government of the Stuarts, and had been opposed in the name of the old principles. Then at the end of the 18th century came the cry for Parliamentary reform followed by the challenge of the French Revolution. It was a period of great peril, but England got through it without a revolution and embarked on a period of peaceful reform with the Reform Act of 1832, and it was claimed that she did so owing to the enlightenment and ultimately the leadership of men like Charles James Fox and Earl Grey of the Reform Bill who had learnt their principles in the opposition to George III and drew on the old Whig sources of inspiration.

The pattern seemed to be continuous, so much so that Macaulay believed that England did not have a destructive revolution in 1848 because she had a 'preserving revolution' in 1688. In due course Whiggery was replaced by Liberalism, but it seemed that the old pattern naturally emerged into the politics of the Anti-Corn Law League and ultimately of Gladstone, so that a myth developed which portrayed English history as the progressive vindication and unfolding of the same principles as a result of the conflict of the same forces mysteriously prolonged through the ages.

There was truth in this myth, and what truth there was is important. It is certainly possible to believe nowadays that important principles have been worked out in English history, and that they relate closely to the maintenance of the freedom of the individual. But no one could now accept the historical framework into which the myth used to be cast. The old interpretation of Saxon institutions was largely imaginary. Much of the medieval evidence was given an anachronistic significance. The issue between the Stuarts and their Parliaments was by no means so simple, nor was what was right and wrong in that quarrel so clearly established by precedent or principle as used to be asserted. The case against George III and the case for the Anti-Corn League had been allowed to pass straight from the contemporary partisan statements of one party to a bitterly contested quarrel into history without any attempt to test the facts on which they were supposed to rest. Even the nature of the Reform Bill of 1832 had been partly misunderstood. Certainly the change it had effected had been exaggerated, and justice had not normally been done to the contribution of any of the men who might from time to time have been adversaries of the Whigs.

In due course this historic framework disintegrated under historical criticism. Various scholars reshaped the old picture of pre-conquest and medieval England. A revision of the one-sided view of the 17th century conflict may be said to have started with the work of S. R. Gardiner. Sir Lewis Namier demolished the Whig interpretation of the actions of George III, and so on. But the fact that so much of the old myth has been demolished is not so significant for present purposes as the fact that it dominated the minds of men for over two centuries, and some of the men who were so dominated were considerable scholars. Henry Hallam who ranks equal with Macaulay as the greatest of the early 19th century Whig historians was a considerable scholar. Bishop Stubbs who was, in his way, a later exponent of the myth was a very considerable scholar. Indeed the continued survival of the myth through the times of Stubbs is one of the most interesting and significant facts in its history. Of course it altered its content as men learnt more and approached history in a more sophisticated fashion. But it still retained its hold on the minds of men, indeed it was largely later 19th century historians who converted that very equivocal, essentially medieval, character Simon de Montfort into a forward-looking Liberal-minded statesman with a profound understanding of the virtues of representative government.[1]

It is useful to study this matter in relation to a myth which is no longer generally accepted, at least not in the form in which it existed in the days of its power. In such a case it is easier to stand outside it and study the assumptions which those, who were influenced by the myth, unconsciously made, and the way these were eroded by further study. It has, however, to be remembered that in spite of its strength, and its longevity, this myth was one which was peculiarly easy to criticize. Its validity depended on the purposes which had been served by certain institutions in specified periods and the ways in which

[1] On this remarkable conversion see C. H. Knowles, *Simon de Montfort 1265–1965*, Historical Association Pamphlet [G.60] (1965).

they had worked. If these things had been misunderstood then the myth had to be abandoned, or at least drastically modified. It was a matter upon which there could be concentrated research. Even where the critics had to take a rather wider sweep as did Sir Lewis Namier with his enquiry into the behaviour and interests of minor 18th century political characters, or the 19th century critics with their studies of constituency politics and party organization, the research was practicable and within easily defined limits. ,

It is otherwise when the myth itself turns on the condition, behaviour and motives of very large groups and classes. This may involve the use of evidence which is both technical and uncertain, and historical problems of greater difficulty than the nature of the precedents on which the 17th century monarchy or Parliament based its case, or even the meaning of an admittedly difficult document like Magna Carta. Yet it is these social myths about classes which are at the moment most likely to affect the generic statements which are admitted into history.

Even, however, when it is not within the power of the reader of history to criticize a myth himself, it is important for him to recognize, if he can, what are the historical myths which have been most likely to affect in one way or another particular issues in history, and also for that matter men's views on some of the problems of contemporary politics. It is also important, if possible, to recognize what myth may have influenced the mind of any historians whose work may be being used. Even if his mind may not have been dominated by the myth itself he may be of the generation of historians who reacted most violently against it, a fact which may have strongly biased his mind in the other direction. In fact it might almost be said that every historical myth develops in due course an anti-myth as a shadow, and this may have an equally distractive effect on the minds of scholars.

The fact that a myth has helped to shape the mind of a scholar by no means implies that his work may be disregarded. It may even have added to its value. A myth may very well have given coherence to what would otherwise have been chaotic and meaningless, and it may give an insight into human affairs which those who are beyond its influence would be likely to miss. It is however always necessary to consider to what extent such a myth may have determined the conditions on which an enquiry may have been undertaken, to what extent it may have suggested facts and explanations for which there is not sufficient evidence.

If it is impossible to reject a general statement because it was framed under the inspiration of a theory of history or an historical myth, it is even more impossible to reject generic or general statements which are founded not upon individual research, the enumeration of facts and the use of mathematics, but upon *impression*. Nor would it be reasonable to try to do so. After all in the ordinary affairs of life the general opinions which men accept are normally founded upon general impressions and not upon detailed research, and the quantities and proportions into which they divide their matter are usually too imprecise to be used for any mathematical calculation. Men have not time to do detailed research into all that they want to talk about, or in relation to which they wish to act. Nor probably in many cases would the material for research be easily available. All this is as true of history and of historians as it is of ordinary affairs and ordinary men. Whatever the modern tendency in historical research, in the ordinary course of business historians will continue to produce general statements based solely upon impression and they will continue to be of great value to the users of history.

Indeed to refuse to accept the testimony of such statements would be impossible, for it would mean turning one's back on the view of the past which one uses every day. As was said in an earlier chapter our view of the past is not just a view of what happens to be there. It is a landscape which has been formed by a number of historians through whose eyes we see, and on whose impressions we must rely. If we refused to use these impressions the past would be colourless, meaningless and incoherent, and we should not be nearer to grips with reality, we should be further off from it. We should be refusing the services of those who have been willing to exercise on our behalf a power which may be fallible but upon the use of which a very large amount of human knowledge necessarily rests. For the power of meditating upon a series of separate facts and forming a general opinion on them is, in fact, one of the most valuable and mysterious which the human mind possesses. When it is raised to its highest power, it is rightly called genius, but many men and women who could lay no claim to anything like genius have possessed it in some degree. When it is well developed in an historian it is called the 'historical imagination', that is the power of imagining the conditions, the men, the actions of a past period as a convincing whole distilled from the disparate evidence available.

Such powers can reveal much that the process of detailed research, however ingeniously its results may be manipulated by mathematics, can never reveal. This is particularly true of the personal experiences of human beings and the things which have moved their minds and spirits. Men's actions can be the subject of detailed research and enumerated, so, with much less certainty, can the influences which possibly affected their actions and so can their words. But what went on in their minds escapes exact scrutiny and classification. It can only be known by inference, and to understand it, if it is to be understood at all, intuition and imagination are necessary; it can never be discovered by means of the mere accumulation of detail however massive that accumulation may be.

This is, however, really true about many other enquiries which are in fact based on the record of a large number of separate facts. Something other than mathematics is needed to give the result significance and meaning. Without this factor they will remain a mere heap of separate facts, that barren detritus which is so often the only result of much wasted effort expended in research. This necessary factor is essentially the same as the faculty which enables a man to form an opinion out of his impressions after simply meditating upon a subject. There is every advantage in accumulating as much exact information as is possible about members of a group, there is the strongest case for doing this systematically and for using mathematics to elucidate the result. But the final creative act which forges a significant general statement must normally be supplied by the imagination.

It is dangerous to be misled on this point. It is very easy to be persuaded that some conclusion is the inevitable result of an uncompromised mathematical calculation, when in fact other factors have co-operated to produce a result which mathematics by itself could not produce. It is possible that these factors may have been introduced by assumptions supplied, or the conclusion forecast, by some historical theory or myth. If so it is important to realize the fact. It may be natural that such theories or myths should be introduced to make sense of what would otherwise be inchoate, but it is important to know what is happening, and with what general ideas one is confronted. Or it is possible that the final conclusion is in the last resort the product of someone's creative imagination. If so it is important to realize this too, since, however remarkable its powers the working of the imagination is subjective. It can reveal what nothing else can reveal, but it is not like a mathematical calculation. No one else can go over the steps by which the result was reached to check it and to see where an error has possibly been introduced into the process. It is, of course, possible for some one else to look at the material and to say, if it seems so, that the first observer's result was wrong. That judgement will however be subjective also, whether one accepts it will depend partly on one's sense of probability and partly on the personal question which of the two observers in fact one trusts.

The less systematic the research, the larger the extent to which it depends upon intuition, the more important this personal question may be. This will not necessarily be offset by the fact that the writer cites quotations and instances to support his opinion. There is often a misunderstanding here owing to the fact that many people think that what will suffice for an *example* will suffice for a *proof*. This is not so. All that can be required of an example is that it should honestly and accurately fit the facts which it is being used to exemplify. But no more need be asked of it. If however it is contended that what is presented is a *proof* of the truth of a general statement then there must be some reason to believe that the incidents, quotations, facts—whatever it is that is proffered—are also representative, that is that they fairly represent all the possible cases, which the general statement purports to describe, or at least so large a number of them as to ensure the general truth of the statement. It is rare for a single instance to be capable of doing this, nor is the general truth of a statement likely to be proved by the citation of two or even three examples when the cases under discussion run into hundreds and thousands, or even for that matter into tens and twenties.

This might seem to be sufficiently obvious, but in fact readers very often accept the truth of a statement endorsed, by one or two examples without any guarantee that the examples are representative. No doubt in many cases they are wise to do so, but they should realize upon what they are relying. For in these cases they are relying upon a man not upon a calculation; they are relying upon the integrity, the perception, the sense of reality of the man who made the generalization not, if there is no guarantee that the examples are representative, upon any objective proof that the generalization is true.

The same kind of personal equation must be the measure of the value of what is called 'literary evidence'. Much of what is important about the conditions that prevailed in the past can be learnt, indeed can only be learnt, from the writing of contemporaries. Letters, diaries, travel books, works of fiction can, consciously or unconsciously, say something of what the world of the past looked like to those who saw it with living eyes, and what they reveal has a greater assurance of reality than can have any reconstruction by any later historian, however ingenious or imaginative he may be. How important and vivid such a contribution to historical knowledge can be may be realized from the impact of those who have contributed contemporary pictures of English life at various dates—the writers of the Paston letters, Pepys, Baxter, Defoe at least as far as his reports on his travels go, Pastor Moritz, Cobbett—to name but a few of those who appear before the great mass of 19th century diarists, letter writers and novelists. Their testimony is of incomparable value; yet they are all human beings and, however vividly they wrote, they had the limitations of human beings. Their impressions may be coloured by prejudice, stultified by ignorance or incapacity, partial through lack of opportunity. What they wrote may be only true of one particular group of men and women, or of one limited locality, or of one very ephemeral moment of time, and it may be very dangerous to yield to the temptation to generalize from what they recorded in order to describe the conditions that commonly prevailed in any epoch.

For these reasons however long a witness may have matured in the grave, however convenient or telling his testimony or for that matter however august his literary reputation, he must be cross-questioned like any other witness. The questions to be asked must be the normal ones; what were his opportunities of observing what he reported, or the likelihood of his understanding what he observed? How perceptive was he likely to have been, and what were his blind spots? What was his bias and the probability of his telling the truth? Has anyone tampered with the report after it has been recorded? Do we possess a selection from it, or the whole? Has it been published without alterations or excisions?

It may not be possible to get answers to all these questions. If so it is, as always, important to know that they have not been answered. In many cases the answers may be complicated, for they may be different for different parts of a witness's work. Take Charles Dickens as an instance. Any who has worked on English 19th century sources will I believe have recognized that Charles Dickens was not only an observer of genius but also often one of unusual accuracy. When he described what might happen in a law court or what could be seen of the House of Commons by a man looking scornfully down from the reporters' seats in the gallery, when he drew his portraits of the people he knew well, middle to lower class people of London and South Eastern England, he produced pictures which the most diligent research can confirm, although by itself it could never have created them. At times they may seem to us to be extravagant, but the untouched truth seems often enough to have had an extravagance which shews through the most prosaic records.

However in using Dickens it is important to be selective. There were parts of the country he did not know well. He seems to have only known the manufacturing districts of the Midlands and North as an intermittent observer. It is probably for this reason that, though *Hard Times* is an interesting sociological tract, the workmen in it do not seem to be quite real, nor do they seem to correspond with such evidence as exists. Not only his local knowledge, but his sympathies and interests seem to have had their limits. He does not seem to have wanted to understand the aristocracy. Partly for that reason, though he could describe the weaknesses of the existing system of government in Britain with great brilliance from outside, he could not see clearly the inwardness of the difficult contemporary problems of politics and administration, for the control of both was largely in the hands of the aristocracy. Sometimes indeed his very strong radical prejudices overcame his excellent common sense, and at times the literary conventions of the day were too much for him and he resorted to passages of melodrama and sentimentalism, which are inherently false whatever their subject matter.

It is therefore necessary not to be dazzled by Dickens' great name and great powers, but to use him, as it is necessary to use other witness, with discretion. This is also true of a man who strongly influenced Dickens. Thomas Carlyle could also be an observer of brilliance. His most remarkable pictures are, indeed, of individuals, for they are the pictures in his letters and journals of the various people he met in person in London and elsewhere. But there is much knowledge to be gained about the ethos of the society of Carlyle's early manhood by those who can distil a coherent meaning from the turmoil of *Sartor Resartus* and some of the tracts which immediately followed it. Nevertheless Carlyle also had his geographical and social limitations. He knew the literary, and in some part the aristocratic, life of London, and he knew the peasant life of the area round Ecclefechan, but he does not seem to have known much of the counties which lie between London and Scotland, and anyone turning to his tract on *Chartism* to find out what was moving the Chartists of South Lancashire, Staffordshire and the West Riding of Yorkshire is likely to be misled or disappointed.

None of this should be particularly surprising. It merely means that any literary witness, Dickens, Carlyle or even Shakespeare, should be treated critically like any other witness. There is however one question which when confronted with literary evidence it is unusually important to ask. It is this. If the passage cited were replaced into its appropriate position in the work from which it has been drawn, would it still bear the same meaning and support the same implications as the man, who has cited it, has attributed to it? It is necessary to ask this, partly because of the very common abuse of quotations, which are often enough used by people who believe they know who the authors were but have no idea, and seem to care little, in what circumstances the words they cite were first used; partly because even conscientious people without an historical training apparently find it difficult to realize how drastically the historical context of a statement can affect its meaning, and partly because perfunctory writers still apparently believe that one or two quotations selected at convenience from the works of the eminent dead are a satisfactory solution to the difficult problem of how to sum up the actions, the ways of thought, or the condition of a large number of people of whom they themselves know little and about whom they are not going to trouble themselves to find out more.

So much for the general statements about groups and situations founded upon impressions. Alongside of them must be placed the general statements founded upon the *systematic examination* of details, their enumeration and possibly the use of mathematics to elucidate the result. It need hardly be repeated that where it is practicable to use these methods and where the subject matter is suitable for them they have great advantages. They impose on the enquiry such objective control as the use of system and mathematics impose. They may suggest possibilities which the unassisted imagination of the researcher would not have suggested, and they shew clearly the proportions of things, a matter on which personal impressions are notoriously deceptive.

Of recent years there has been an increasing tendency among historians to use these methods when they wished to make generic statements about large groups. But the development is slow because the practice of these methods is necessarily difficult and time consuming.

A necessary preliminary is likely to be extensive, accurate and laborious research into matters whose significance may seem to be confined to very restricted localities and into the lives and activities of men and women who were in their day exceedingly obscure. To conduct such research often requires some training in the technicalities of particular records, which to the uninstructed might be meaningless or deceptive. When the material is assembled there must be an increased use of what is called 'quantification', which in this context must be held to mean the expression of historical statements in exact quantities, if that is possible, in statistics. To interpret the result of quantification a certain amount of mathematics will be necessary, particularly perhaps of the use of algebra, a convenience which too many people leave behind them at school. It may also be necessary to learn to use the technique of the punched card and the computer, methods which historians of an older generation feel to be foreign to their art, and in themselves repugnant.

Certainly the increased use of these methods promises a most interesting revolution in history. Yet it is important to recognize that the tendency of which they are the culmination is not new. As far as England is concerned it dates back to the 17th century. In England the use of detail, exactly observed, as a basis for historical generalization might be considered to have its father in Sir Henry Spelman who lived from 1564 to 1641. Quantification in matters concerning human beings might be said to begin with John Graunt whose dates are 1620–74 and Sir William Petty whose dates are 1623–87. An early exponent was Gregory King, 1648–1712, who made a notable attempt to determine the size of the population of England.

This beginning in the 17th century is significant, for this tendency is in reality part of the scientific revolution. That revolution led to the substitution of exact knowledge for traditional assertions, loose estimates and guesswork, to the attempt to replace *a priori* judgements by induction and the attempt to use where possible mathematical methods to control the subject matter under discussion; and this change in the methods of historical research is the embodiment of those tendencies. It carries with it the same promise as other departments of the scientific revolution and the same dangers, the temptation to exaggerate the area which its achievements have brought under control or to pretend to apply its methods to subject matter which is unsuited for them or is not ready to receive them. As with the rest of the scientific revolution the advance in the 19th century was very great and the 20th century is beginning to reap the increase.

The reasons for the advance in the 19th century were

various. Under the inspiration of German and French scholars British historians greatly extended their use of exact and detailed scholarship, particularly perhaps in their treatment of constitutional and institutional history. At the same time there was an increasing interest in the economic and social background to history and also in the exact statistical analysis of contemporary society. In the 18th century such analysis had been made difficult by the absence of reliable figures and records. In that matter England seems to have been worse off than France, or Scandinavia, but from whatever source reliable figures were hard to come by. Anyone who reads the work of Malthus on population will realize how severely he was hampered by the lack of reliable vital statistics. But from the beginning of the 19th century a change began. In 1801 there was the first census. It was not very reliable, but it was the beginning of an increasingly reliable enumeration of the population at ten years' intervals throughout the century. In 1836 there was passed an act for the civil registration of births, marriages and deaths so that from 1837 reasonable vital statistics began to be available. Meanwhile a number of other enquiries, some official, some conducted by private statistical societies, were accumulating a good deal of other numerical data, not all of it equally reliable.

Towards the end of the 19th century and in the 20th century the results of detailed research and of quantification began to bite deep into the prevailing myths of history and in some cases to supply a new general picture more firmly based on methodical research. Using the tools of exact scholarship J. H. Round attacked many of the traditional assumptions of English constitutional history with unnecessary rancour, but with success. T. F. Tout built up his picture of the way in which the medieval monarchy had worked from a careful study of the details of its administrative processes. The same careful study of detail enabled A. F. Pollard and his successors to build up a new and much more reliable picture of the work and achievement of the Tudors. The study of the behaviour and motives of the minor characters in politics enabled Sir Lewis Namier to revolutionize some of the important developments in British politics associated with George III. The study of what actually happened in a large number of constituencies has helped to put the results of the Reform Act of 1832 into better perspective and modified the picture of the politics of the next twenty years that followed and the crisis of the repeal of the Corn Laws.

Economic and social history became increasingly important as the 19th century proceeded. To a large extent economic history from the first necessarily made use of such statistics as trade returns, while between 1866 and 1887 Thorold Rogers developed the history of prices. Nevertheless in the sphere of what might be called social history historians were still accustomed to use generalizations about the conditions, or the intentions of large classes, which were largely based upon impressions endorsed by quotations which were by no means necessarily representative, as the work of Mr and Mrs Hammond goes to shew. In his great *Economic History of Modern Britain*, the first volume of which was published in 1926, Sir John Clapham challenged some of the most important of these generalizations. It could not be claimed that he was a pioneer in the methods he used, but it seems possible that his book was a turning point, for though it has been effectively challenged in its turn, it has been challenged on the ground of his use of statistics. No one could now, honestly, go back to the methods he criticized.

What has happened is therefore the result of a movement which has a reasonably long history. Nevertheless it is as well to realize that the full extent of this revolution as it affected generic statements about large groups or classes was not fully realized by the generation of historians which has just passed away. This was not only true of Mr and Mrs Hammond; it was also true of an historian of the calibre of G. M. Trevelyan.

Trevelyan was prepared to make general statement of the old sort based on his impression of the facts. This was, it is true, formed after reading all that he could lay his hands upon till in his own phrase 'he could burst', but without a systematic enquiry into individual cases and of course without any attempt at quantification. His knowledge of history, particularly of the history of Britain in the 17th century, was so great and his instinctive understanding of the realities of the past so strong as to give the pictures he painted as a result of this process peculiar value. They are no doubt of greater value than would be likely to have been produced by the mere accumulation of the results of research into detail by a duller man. Nevertheless they are without the check which a realization of the importance of detailed research and exact analysis might have suggested to him, if he had had the advantage of living a generation or two later, and from time to time the limitations of his methods reveal themselves in a loose use of such phrases as 'middle class' or 'working class', or in his easy acceptance of a partisan tradition which has not in other hands survived the test of a detailed analysis. These failures can, perhaps, be seen most clearly in his work on the 19th century on the problems of which his touch is less certain than it is when he is dealing with the 17th century.

Of recent years the movement towards the increased use of research into detail, of quantification and exact social research has received an important fillip from three sources—from the development of the techniques of sociology, particularly in the United States, from the example of a remarkable series of French demographers and from the opportunities supplied by the use of computers. For computers have made a number of calculations possible and easy that without their help would have been impracticable or so burdensome and lengthy that they would never have been undertaken. At the moment the use of computers by historians has been I suppose most pronounced in work on demographical problems and in the analysis of economic growth and of social structure, but already there has been an overspill into political, particularly electoral, history.

There is no doubt their use will be pressed further. Indeed there is little doubt it will be pressed too far. For men will forget that no hole in the punched card can exactly represent, and no computing machine completely elucidate, what has gone on in a man's mind. Nevertheless the methods of detailed research and quantification with whatever mechanical aids may be available, are likely to be so valuable, and to be the deciding factor in so many questions, that it will be necessary for the serious student to come to terms with them.

In order to do this it would if possible be desirable to learn something about the technique of using statistics. The procedures which are likely to be needed in the analysis of historical problems are no doubt for a mathematician relatively simple, but for those of us who have never learnt anything about statistics and left behind whatever we had of mathematics when we left the middle forms at our school, they are going to present pitfalls and difficulties. Indeed quantification is in the future going to be so important in all walks of life, that it is to be hoped that in all schools some training in its use may be given to all intelligent children whatever subject they are taking. It should not be difficult to arrange such training in connection with a course on historical criticism.

Those of us who have not received such training must be content with reading, and trying to understand, some of the simpler literature on the subject.[1] But even if we cannot get very far with this there is at least one lesson we can learn. We can learn not to be afraid of statistics. Statistics are, after all, no more than useful ways of summarizing information. They are the servants of mankind; they must never be promoted to the position of master with the right to demand unquestioning obedience. By themselves they prove nothing, men and women prove conclusions with the aid of statistics. In fact they are no more than tools, and whether they deceive, mislead, or reveal what is important and true depends on the use that is made of them by fallible, and potentially dishonest, human beings.

Certainly they can mislead and deceive. In an age in the thought and discussions of which quantification plays an increasingly important part a statement tricked out in that appearance of accuracy which exact figures give can lay claim to an authority to which it has no right. Perhaps good examples of this are the very confident reports of the successful results of the British bombing offensive against Germany in the early years of the last war. They encouraged the continuance of a policy which was very expensive in human life, and might conceivably, since it made large demands on resources desperately needed elsewhere, have led to defeat. Yet they were completely misleading.[2] In this case the deception was innocent, the self-deception of honest, well-intentioned and intelligent

---

[1] A useful book might be M. J. Moroney, *Facts from Figures* (a Pelican Original) (1963). See also W. O. Aydelotte, *Amercian Historical Review*, April 1966, 'Quantification in History'.

[2] C. Webster and N. Frankland, *The Strategic air offensive against Germany* (1961), Vol. I, pp. 218–32, pp. 299–306.

men. But statistics will not only be used by the honest and well-intentioned, and in the hands of men whose honesty is not perhaps beyond question and whose intentions are kept out of sight they can be dangerous weapons. Perfectly irrelevant, or inaccurate, figures have sometimes been introduced into an argument with deadly effect, an effect which is enhanced by a natural human tendency to be impressed by what appears to be a formidably accurate statement without troubling to consider what in reality it proves, and not to verify it, but to believe that someone else must have done so.

Even when the figures are relevant and correct they may still mislead. This is particularly likely to happen when no facts are given to shew their proportionate importance, as when the number of cases in which a certain condition is revealed without giving the maximum number of cases in which it could occur. An example of this kind of deception is sometimes to be found in discussions on road safety, when the number of accidents in a given year is compared with that in an earlier year without giving the increase in the number of cars on the road. No doubt the intentions are good, but the suggestions about the facts are misleading. The same kind of deception can be conveyed through a graph. If the zero point is left out of a graph, or no adequate scale is introduced, it may be impossible to realize the proportionate importance of the change which is being recorded. But there are other ways in which a graph can deceive. For instance a short section of a long curve can be given with the misleading suggestion that the trend of the rest of the curve is the same, or when the trend line has been plotted from very widely scattered points the points can be erased and the trend line alone be left.

Deliberate dishonesty is not normally to be looked for in an history book, but carelessness or misunderstanding in the use of figures is always possible and it is important for the student of history to be on his guard. Of peculiar importance in historical matters is the proportionate significance of a set of figures. For instance if it is said that the increase in urbanization or in child labour affected the death rate in England and Wales in the late 18th century or early 19th century it is necessary to ask what proportion of the population was in fact in any year being drawn into towns and how many of the children of the

C.H.—7

country were in fact being drawn into factories. It is also important to be sure that all the statistics which might bear on the figures which are being used are given. For instance if figures were given to demonstrate the death rate of workers in a particular industry it might be necessary not only to give the comparable figures for other men in the same age and income group but also those who lived in the same districts and under the same conditions but who followed different occupations.

The mistakes or misrepresentations which may vitiate the value of statistics may not have been the fault of those who incorporated the statistics into an argument. They may have crept in at an earlier stage of the transaction. Someone must have collected the facts on which any statistics are based. Someone must in all probability have collated the facts which they collected and someone edited the results for publication. All the people who did these things were fallible and their failures may have affected the statistics for which they were responsible. It may therefore be important to learn something about them, or at least about the way in which they worked, before accepting what they produced.

Take, as an instance, the history of the British census. The collection of the facts on which the first census was based in 1801 was in the hands of the Overseers of the Poor. No doubt they did their best, but there is no reason to believe that they were peculiarly well-equipped for a task which was in any case without precedent. They were also hampered by the nature of the English parish and the unmanageably large populations to be found in some urban parishes. Nor since householders did not themselves receive schedules to fill in and no names were recorded, has it ever been possible to check the results of their work. In the circumstances it is unlikely that it was absolutely accurate, indeed it seems probable that they underestimated the size of the population. After 1840 conditions were better. The technique of taking the census had improved and various institutions had come into existence which enabled the work to be accurately done. The reform of the poor law in 1834 had provided Poor Law unions which were more satisfactory units for the purposes of the census than the old parishes; the Municipal Reform Act of 1835 had provided reliable officials for those areas which it touched. Most important of all an act of

1836 passed to make provision for the civil registration of births, marriages and deaths, instituted local Registrars all over the country under whom the enumerators could work.

The census in 1841 is therefore better than those which preceded it. Nevertheless even in 1841 exact ages were only given for persons under fifteen, after that ages were only given in quinquennial periods. The relationships of the members of the same household were not given and the birth places of the people enumerated often only sketchily given. In 1851 things were better; even so a certain amount of special knowledge is necessary to interpret the famous religious census of that year and to understand what might be the relation between the published figures and the numbers of people who did in particular cases actually attend Church on Census Sunday. In not a few cases those numbers are in fact irrecoverable.[1]

No doubt those who habitually use the census returns know all about these complications, and allow for them, but anyone who did not, and who did not trouble to ask how the published figures had been compiled, might believe that they were a good deal more authoritative and explicit than in fact they are.

However leaving aside the possibility of incomplete or inaccurate recording, or deceptive editing, some statistics present another possible cause for misunderstanding. It may spring from the nature of the units on which the figures are based. Clearly an overall figure may be deceptive if in fact like has not been added to like to make up the sum. For instance if in an enquiry into social conditions it is desired to estimate the number of shopkeepers in a particular area at a particular date it will be deceptive if in the lists which are used under the heading of 'greengrocer' there are numbered not only the proprietors of greengrocers' shops but the assistants in them also, and stall holders and barrow boys into the bargain. Added together they will not make a socially coherent group and an argument based on the belief that they are such will not be worth much.

[1] See A. J. Taylor, *British Medical Journal*, 1951, Vol. 1, p. 715 ff. 'The taking of the Census, 1801–1951'. L. J. Hector, *The Amateur Historian*, Vol. 1, No. 6, June-July 1955, p. 174 ff. 'The census returns of 1841 and 1851'. I have learnt much about the religious census from Mr D. M. Thompson, Fellow of Fitzwilliam College, Cambridge.

David Thompson who became a first-class church historian. He as I did the (20") Documentary Historian A. Newcastle published :- 2007 !

In some of the older records it may not be easy to be sure what some of the entries mean or whether they always mean the same thing. For instance the older names for occupations, and for status, may not be easy to translate into intelligible realities and may not mean the same in all parts of the country. There is the same kind of problem with regard to the record of diseases before the possibility of effective diagnosis. I am told that when 'leprosy' is referred to in ancient records it may in fact mean any one of a number of skin infections. Certainly 'fever' in early 19th century records covers a number of diseases. Clearly there are the possibilities of misconstruction here. Clearly quantification could be deceptive, if the numbers used were not based on the careful analysis and accurate definition of what is to be quantified.

The task of definition may not be easy, particularly when what is to be quantified must be isolated by accurate social or economic analysis, and the categories chosen may be controversial, or at least questionable. It is therefore desirable that, before he uses the results of quantification, the reader of history should if possible give some thought to the way in which this work has been done. This may not be too easy if the documents on which the calculation is based are ones for the understanding of which expert technical knowledge is required. But he can be on his guard against such imprecise and misleading classifications as those to which the names given to social and economic types very easily lead, and against tautology, such practices that is as the careful definition of a class of people who are intrinsically likely to do something to be followed by a mathematical proof that most of them in fact do do it. This is a practice which can sometimes lie hidden behind a formidable façade of quasi-scientific terms.

There is another question which the reader should consider, that is whether the number of cases examined will support the conclusions which it is intended to base upon the results of the enquiry. It is obviously possible that the enquiry should be too small in scope to support general statements about the larger sections of the community which may be under discussion. There is, indeed, a tendency to err in this direction in research in social history. Such research is often laborious and tedious and there is a strong temptation to reach an interesting conclusion before such a conclusion is justifiable. But it is also possible to allow the base of an enquiry to be too wide for the conclusions which it is supposed to support. To give an instance which has been mentioned before, if too large a section of the community is taken into account when the economic condition of a class is in question then the average standard attained by the whole section may have little or no relevance to the normal standard of life of large sections of the class.

This forms part of the case against Sir John Clapham's claim that there was a general improvement of working class conditions in the first half of the 19th century. It is said that he took so large a section of the community as the basis for his figures that he ignored considerable sections of the working class whose conditions had in fact deteriorated, as it was also said that he did not take account of the incidence of unemployment, sickness or old age since those who suffered from these things were excluded from his figures by the terms of his enquiry.

What should be the scope of the enquiry, what should be included in it and how its subject matter should be analysed and categorized are questions for the personal decision of whoever it is that is conducting the enquiry. No doubt these decisions are often dictated by the object of the enquiry. But they may require the solution of some difficult problems, and, to judge by the controversy about Sir John Clapham's results, it is possible that the preconceptions of an historian and his acceptance or rejection of a particular historical myth may influence the way a particular historian may solve these problems. If they do they will also influence his results however massive and accurate his calculations may be.

The same thing is true of the assumptions he may make in order to interpret his results. It may not be easy in all cases to detect what these assumptions are. They can slip into the calculation so naturally that neither the writer nor the reader will have realized what has happened, or they may seem so obvious that it is not easily realized that they are assumptions at all. Even so they may be mistaken. There is an example from classical archaeology of a conclusion which very many scholars reached as the result of a mistaken assumption. The example is the more instructive because the assumption is one that is very often made, but which is in fact always dangerous, the assumption that if in a large mass of evidence there is no mention of something it did not exist. There is apparently no mention of riding in Homer, and for a very long time the generally accepted conclusion was that the Greeks of the heroic age went about in chariots but did not ride. Unfortunately several Mycenaean clay statuettes have been found of men who are palpably riding. The argument that the beasts which they are riding are donkeys not horses and that this is not 'real riding' is not convincing.[1]

In some cases the nature of the assumptions which must be made before any figures which exist can be interpreted raises very difficult and very controversial historical problems. A good example of this are the assumptions which must be made to establish from what figures are available what was the size of the population of England in the 17th and 18th centuries. The first census was in 1801. As has been said it was most probably an underestimate of the population of the country, but from that date increasingly accurate figures are available. Before 1801 a variety of records exist, the most important of which are the records of baptisms, weddings and burials in the parish register. It is clear that these do not present at any date the complete figures for all births, unions and deaths in the country, but what is the margin of error? What figure should be added to the figures obtained from the parish registers to obtain a reasonably reliable estimate of the figures for the whole of England?

An obvious way of tackling this problem is to compare the figures from the parish registers with the reliable figures when they do exist and to work out from that comparison a margin of error which can be used to correct the figures for the years before 1801. At one time this method seems to have satisfied the demographers, but it contains an obvious flaw. There is no real reason to assume that the size of the error was constant in all the years before reliable figures were available for comparison. Its size would depend on the effect of a number of different factors which both varied from time to time, and differed in importance in different parts of the country. The proportion of the population included in the registers would

[1] I owe this example to the kindness of Mr F. H. Sandbach of Trinity College and Dr F. A. Stubbings of Emmanuel College.

depend for instance on the numbers of non-conformists in any parish, their attitude at any given time to baptism and marriage in the Parish Church and burial in the Parish churchyard. It would also depend on the attitude of the parochial clergy towards them, and the care and inclusiveness with which the parish register was kept. There is every reason to believe that these factors were never of the same order throughout the country and did not remain the same throughout the 18th and into the 19th century. Demographers have therefore dismissed the assumption that the error was constant; it has been claimed that there was a decisive change about 1780. It is unnecessary to discuss here whether that date is satisfactory. To a non-expert its choice would appear still to depend on assumptions about the answers to a number of contingent problems on which there has as yet not been sufficient detailed research to endorse any answer. However the point of importance here is not whether any particular estimate is satisfactory, but the fact that it is impossible to estimate from these figures what the population was at any date with any hope of accuracy unless a number of difficult historical questions are answered, and that it is very tempting to assume what that answer should be without sufficient evidence to justify the assumption.[1]

An historian's personal judgement may therefore slip into a calculation, which appears at first sight to depend on the most chaste and impersonal use of quantification, both when the original problem is defined and when the result is interpreted. It may also intrude itself into what is in many ways the most interesting and important use of statistics, the comparison of two sets of figures to see whether there is a significant correspondence, or a significant lack of correspondence between them. Indeed the nature of this calculation increases the number of the problems which any use of figures must entail, and therefore of the issues which may be decided at the personal discretion of the researcher. For in addition to the questions which each set of figures may raise there is the question

[1] For a discussion of the sources on this subject see the introduction to the 1967 edition of G. T. Griffith, *Population Problems of the Age of Malthus* and *An introduction to English Historical Demography*, Peter Laslett, R. C. C. Eversley, W. A. Armstrong, edited by E. A. Wrigley (1966). Each book has a useful bibliography.

whether the comparison is fair, whether the result is significant and if it is significant in what way it is significant.

A good example of the difficulties involved in such a comparison seems to be provided by some of the attempts to use quantification to test which of the works ascribed to an author were in fact written by him. A count of the number of times certain common words and common constructions are used in the books which are without question his and then a like count is made to test the frequency of the same words and the same constructions in the works under suspicion. If the frequencies are the same then the doubtful works are accepted as being genuine, if they are different then the works are spurious.

The results of this method have been extremely interesting, they are indeed a typical example of the way in which the use of computers can help scholarship. But they have sometimes been controversial, and some of the controversies which have resulted from their use, particularly perhaps from the denial to St Paul of some of the works commonly attributed to him, have brought into relief the difficulties which develop when two different sets of figures are compared and the contingent problems which have to be settled before such a comparison is satisfactory. Only a scholar who was expert in the subject matter of these controversies, and also in the technique of using statistics, could say with any confidence with whom among the various participants the advantage lay; but they are of great interest to a layman since they demonstrate clearly the issues which the use of this method involves. They also appear to demonstrate the resistance which is likely to develop when the use of statistics and the computer is first introduced into a branch of study which is not accustomed to them.[1]

[1] See A. Q. Morton and J. McLennan, *Christianity and the Computer* (1964), and for the controversy which ensued, *The Expository Times*, Vol. 76 (1964–5), pp. 17–18, 176 and 367–70, and Vol. 77 (1965–6), p. 116 ff., and A. Q. Morton, 'The Authorship of Greek Prose', *Journal of the Royal Statistical Society* (Ser. A), Vol. 128, p. 169 ff. See also M. C. Brown, *The Authentic Writings of St Ignatius. A study of Linguistic Criteria.* (Duke University Press, Durham N. C., 1963), and F. Mosteller and D. J. Wallace, 'Inference in Authorship Problems', *Journal of the American Statistical Association*, Vol. 50, pp. 275–300. (On certain papers in the *Federalist* whose authorship is disputed). I owe these references in large part to the kindness of Professor H. Chadwick of Oxford.

Some comparisons are certainly significant. Important results can come from noting the relationship between two sets of variables. For instance between 1848 and 1854 Dr John Snow, an eminent physician in London, turned his attention to the incidence of cases of cholera and he discovered that if a map of the various houses where cholera had been diagnosed was compiled they were heavily grouped in certain streets, and particularly in certain houses, which shared the same water supply. A positive relationship was established between the water supplied by particular water companies and the incidence of the disease and, though men did not as yet know why this relationship existed, the knowledge so gained saved many lives. Yet in other conditions even though an unquestionable correlation has been established the conclusion to which it led may be pure nonsense. It is well to remember the old joke attributed to Mark Twain that he had worked things out and discovered that more people died in bed than anywhere else. Therefore, said he, it is most dangerous to go to bed.

In fact the comparison by itself may be meaningless, it may be the circumstances which give it meaning and it is possible that it may need some interpreter to say precisely what its meaning and significance is. There is a story told I believe of the poet Calverley when, under the name of Blayds, he was making his first, and in due course unsuccessful, attempt at a University career as an undergraduate at Balliol College, Oxford; though it has no doubt often been told of other young men whose blood was too lively to permit them to remain for long at their books during working hours. 'How is it Mr Blayds,' the Dean of Balliol is reported to have said, 'that whenever I look out of my window you are crossing the Quad?' 'And how is it Mr Dean', said Blayds, 'that whenever I cross the Quad you look out of your window?' No doubt the College authorities decided which was the significant side of this correlation, but such an authoritative settlement is not always available and similar problems about other correlations may raise issues of considerable difficulty and importance. For instance in 19th century Britain there was supposed to be a close correlation between poverty and drunkenness. It is quite probable that there was, but if so that leaves open the problem whether people where poor because they were drunken, or drunken because they were poor.

In the 19th century the prevalent assumption would be that people were poor because they were drunken, in the 20th that they were drunken because they were poor. Each assumption would depend on prevalent assumptions about the nature of poverty. In the middle of the 19th century even people of good will were inclined to believe that, putting aside the results of old age or infancy or illness or undeserved misfortune, poverty was likely to be the fault of those who were poor. It was likely to have been caused by shiftlessness or by bad habits of which drunkenness was the chief. In the 20th century the prevailing assumption is that poverty is the fault of society, and that bad habits, heavy drinking among them, are the results of poverty and the bad conditions which go with poverty. The two conceptions confronted one another in the contrasted attitudes of the Charity Organization Society and the Fabian Society at the turn of the century and came into the open in the proceedings of the Royal Commission on the Poor Law which sat from 1905 to 1909. The difference of approach was of course fundamental and of great importance in the development of public policy. It is true that greater knowledge of the causes of poverty, of the results of unemployment of sickness and of old age had contributed to the new view. But it is difficult to resist the belief that a fundamental difference was one of temperament and tradition and basic social philosophy, so that the same figures, the same correlations might mean different things to different people. If this is so it may be necessary not only to know what figures a man is using but what general ideas will guide him in the interpretation of them. Indeed it might be said that all generalizations about cause and effect in the relation between social conditions and the behaviour of individuals contain within themselves somewhere the dogmas of some social philosophy. It is by no means necessary to reject them on that account, but it is desirable to know what the philosophy may be.

This is desirable not only because it is necessary to know what are the basic assumptions in any man's thought, but also because any generalized view of Society may very well be an over-simplification. Even if what it discloses is correct it may not disclose the whole truth and it is important to see what may lie outside its field of vision. For instance what the old social reformers saw in the relationship between drink and poverty was correct. It was what they did not see, the questions they did not ask, which deceived them in such a way that their diagnosis of the problem of poverty was a false and superficial one. The same thing may be said of those theories of history which have emphasized the extent to which men's economic and class motives have influenced their behaviour in history. These views have in fact provided a valuable insight into human affairs and history has in general been the stronger for them. Nevertheless they over-simplify. By themselves they lead to the neglect of factors in human affairs the importance of which are equal to the influence, in however sophisticated a form it is conceived, of economic interest. It is not however likely that these factors will emerge from statistics based on definitions and interpreted according to the original theory. What has to be done is to ask other questions and reveal other facts, which may perhaps not contradict the original assertions but may shew what truth lies outside them.

The history of the development of one particular historical problem can perhaps demonstrate how the asking of new questions can disclose the full complexity of a situation that had been superficially disposed of. The British Parliament which sat from 1841–7 was largely concerned with the question which imposed duties for the protection of agriculture should be repealed or no. Historians have therefore been interested to work out the relation between the economic interests of members and their votes on this question and others related to it. The first attempts to do this were simple. Members were listed under particular categories—landowner, merchant, manufacturer and so on and the relation of these categories to their votes noted. This seemed to be a satisfactory way of handling the problem until Professor W. O. Aydelotte of Iowa State University instituted a systematic enquiry into all the circumstances of the members of that Parliament. He discovered all that he could about each of them. The information was then recorded on punched cards and put through a computer with the object of discovering the relationship between these factors and a man's voting habits. The first result of this technique was to demonstrate how inadequate were any simple categories for the description of a man's economic position, and how complex his interests might be. He might not only be a landowner but also a shipowner, the director of a railway company, the owner of urban house property. These interests might point in different directions on the issue of the Corn Laws.

However other complications necessarily enter this problem. It is necessary to take account of a member's relation with his constituents, a relationship which varied according to whether he represented a county, a large borough or a pocket borough. For in the electoral conditions of those days whether a member could vote as he liked, or had to pay attention to the wishes of his constituents, depended on the nature of the constituency and who controlled the 'influence' in it. It is also necessary to understand what were his relations to his party and its leader, and whether he, or any member of his family, held, or had the expectation of, a government job.

The resulting picture is complicated. It reveals factors in the situation which could have only been revealed by asking questions of the evidence which may very well not have occurred to those who first gave thought to the matter, and the progressive development of this problem seems to suggest how valuable it may be, when faced with a calculation based on quantification, to consider what issues may lie outside it.

What I have said is not intended to be an account of the technical problems which the process of quantification may present; for that it is necessary to go to the technical books on the use of statistics. It has been intended to suggest that detailed research, the use of statistics and quantification, are like any other methods of research no more than tools in the hands of human beings. How they are used will depend on the human beings who use them, and bias, error or ignorance may vitiate their usefulness as they may vitiate the usefulness of any other intellectual techniques which human beings use. This may be the more serious because these human failings may be effectively concealed behind the apparent objectivity of a mass of figures.

It is therefore important that anyone who uses the results of these methods should be aware of this danger and be prepared to ask with what preconceptions those who did the research approached their task. It is also desirable for him to be ready for another, possibly minor, intellectual nuisance. These methods have been recognized as being 'scientific', and, in so far as they are systematic and depend, where possible, on exact research rather than impression and upon quantification rather than on guesswork, it is to be supposed that they have some right to the use of that rather equivocal word. Unfortunately men have thought to make them seem to be more 'scientific' by inventing for their results a pretentious vocabulary of latinized technical terms. Very often these express no more than could be said in plain speech; sometimes indeed they are the enemies of clear, or honest, thought, for they can conceal very questionable assumptions, or present what are no more than pompous tautologies. It is therefore a useful exercise for a reader who is confronted by this jargon to translate it back into plain English and see what it looks like then. In saying this it is of course necessary to remember that genuine sociologists must use a technical language for which the synonyms, if they existed, would be clumsy and inexact.

When, however, account has been taken of all these reservations the importance of the development of the technique of research into detail, enumeration and quantification can hardly be exaggerated. It is necessary for any student of history to come to terms with this technique. He must learn to note the fact that it has not been used when the circumstances required its use. He must recognize the possibilities it offers, and also how to criticize its use. He must also learn what are the limitations upon it, and in particular that it is no adequate substitute for the historical imagination and the historian's insight. For no accumulation of detail however massive, no mathematical procedures however ingenious, can alone produce the general picture of a group, a situation or a man, any more than a number of lines and dots and splashes of colour can without the direction of the creative power in the mind of an artist produce any other kind of picture.

CONCLUSION

The Critical Historian

THE TIME is now come for me to describe the principles and the habits which I wish to commend. To do this I must sum up what I have tried to say in this book.

I have suggested why I think it important to adopt these principles and habits of mind. No man can escape from history or for long ignore it. There is no lock to anyone's back door. Whether he likes it or not the results of history, or what purport to be the results of history, or opinions coloured by beliefs about history, will invade his life and mind. He must also be prepared for opinions about history or historical experience to have deeply affected the mind of anyone with whom he has dealings. This being so it is the act of a wise man to come to terms with what he cannot evade, and bring it, if he can, under control; that is he must try to get as near as he can to the reality in the history with which he is confronted, to test the cogency of the historical opinions which are likely to influence his mind, or the minds of anyone who is important to him, and perhaps winnow some of the nonsense out of them. It is my case that to do this he must become a *critical historian*.

Obviously the first step in this process must be for him to realize what is at issue. It is not possible for a man to be critical unless he knows what to criticize, nor will anyone take this matter seriously unless he realizes how many and how important are the matters on which history is likely to force its way into his life. Some of these are obvious, some are not. For instance it would be a very stupid man who did not realize that a diplomatic problem or a political tangle could not be understood without some knowledge of the events that led up to it.

But even in these matters there is likely to be a tendency not to realize how much history may be involved, nor how far back it ought to be carried. For instance men have often enough failed to understand the confused and dangerous problems constantly presented by the tangle of nationalities in Eastern Europe because they did not realize that it is not enough to go back to 1945, or 1939, or even 1900, but that it is necessary to understand what happened in the 19th century, and for that matter between the 4th and 12th centuries.

Because they have failed to give full weight to this, diplomatists, politicians and administrators have often enough tragically mismanaged the problem of nationalism, both in that region and elsewhere. But their failures not only emphasize the danger of not taking enough history into account, they have often amply demonstrated another mistake. They did not take a sufficient number of versions of history into account. It is an easy mistake to make, particularly by those who feel that they have reviewed the history in question critically and dispassionately, and conscientiously rejected their own national myth. But to have rejected one's own myth does not guarantee that one has understood anyone else's. Indeed the defect of many anti-myths is that they are apt to be too practical and too ready to reduce the forces which have governed history to the common-sense pursuit of concrete objectives. Conceived in a mood that tries to reject passion, they are apt to play down the element of passion in human affairs, and to lead men to forget in what ways what happened in the past was not only affected by passion, but will be interpreted in terms of passion by contemporaries. Indeed to understand the force of history in everyday life it is necessary for a man not only to have his own view of history, he must try to take account of any other potentially relevant view of history, however absurd it may seem.

To recognize the force of history in current affairs will be to recognize how much historical knowledge is needed to understand the daily newspaper. I believe many people instinctively understand this. Anyone who has engaged in some form of popular adult education will have realized how eagerly many people grasp at any knowledge which may help them to understand what is happening in the world. It is not always very easy for them to gain what they want, for they often do not know where to go for it and in many cases not much seems to have remained from school. Any help that could be given in this matter would certainly be very useful, for clearly newspapers cannot be expected to supply all the knowledge which is necessary to enable the ordinary man or woman to understand the problems whose current phases they record. However, the newspaper has another lesson to teach. It should itself be regarded as a work of historical scholarship. In their reports, in their comments and most of all in their selection of what to put in the paper, the reporters and editors are themselves acting as historians producing their own version of the past. Men and women should learn to recognize them for what they are, and subject them to the same tests and the same kind of criticism as ordinary historians are subjected to.

In all this the significant history will lie reasonably near the surface. There are less obvious routes by which history, or rather opinions about history, may enter men's minds and lie concealed in matter which does not seem to be historical at all. There is, for instance, the colour which memories of history, often very inaccurate and incomplete memories, give to certain words—perhaps the names of countries, Britain, Germany, the United States—or perhaps what present themselves as abstract nouns, Capitalism, Communism, Imperialism. There is, also, the way in which a man's historical experience affects his sense of probability, his choice of the things he deems likely to happen because he believes they have happened before, or the motive which he believes are likely to be entertained because he thinks he knows that men have entertained them before. In all these matters it is important that men and women should realize what is likely to influence their ways of thinking, because it is only if they do this they can bring such influences under some sort of control.

To bring what derives from history under control it is desirable to adopt the basic principles and to make use of the experience of those who have tried to write history. The most important of the historian's principles is a simple one, though it is often disregarded, or partially disregarded. It is a recognition of the fact that what happened in the past has a unique significance because it happened. It may have demonstrated the working of some observed law or the secular application of some eternal principle, and a knowledge of the law, or of the principle, may have helped the historian to understand what happened. But no law and no principle can by themselves say what did happen. To discover that it is necessary to use those laborious, often indecisive, techniques which historians have developed to establish what has happened. This is no doubt unsatisfactory, but there can be no alternative. 'What ought to have been', or 'can be presumed' must never usurp the place of 'what was', and 'what was' can for an historian alone be decisive; it is the only touchstone he may use.

However if that is the historian's principle an historian's experience will certainly teach him how difficult it is for him to be sure that he really does know 'what was' or 'what did happen'. This is in part the result of a difficulty which is present in all knowledge. No report comes directly to the recipient from the facts reported. It is transmitted by some agency and whatever transmits it may modify it. Even if it seems to come direct through the evidence of the senses, they are probably selective and they may distort in some way. Nor has the recipient any certain way of telling to what extent they select or in what ways they may distort. If what is reported has slipped into the past, then memory, as time passes an increasingly uncertain link in the chain, has been interposed into the process of transmission. If it has been related to the recipient by someone else then to the uncertainties of his own methods of knowledge the uncertainties of another and partially unknown personality will have been added.

As is well known these difficulties raise some important and very difficult philosophical problems. It is probably necessary for an historian to disregard them. They cannot be considered in the business of ordinary life, and the same is true of history. Nevertheless as a matter of practical necessity the historian must always remember that he can only see anything that he deals with through the distorting glass of some human personality. And unfortunately there is no common margin of error which can always be assumed to exist on the same points and in the same directions. People differ in the exactitude of their powers of observation and in the kind of things they see or do not see.

In addition to these basic problems any report must also raise those simpler problems which an historian's experience will suggest, as for instance the need to ask such questions as: What is the bias or interest of the reporter? Is his report corroborated? How intelligible is it? What may have happened to it before it reached the historian? Has it been edited or mutilated in any way? There are a good many of these problems, and I have tried to suggest what they are and what questions can with advantage be asked of any evidence. No doubt if these questions are asked the answers to them will on occasion confirm or discredit the information which depends on that evidence, but it is important to realize that in many cases, the results will be indecisive for the simple reason that it will be impossible to cross examine those who are responsible for producing the information. Even so it is still likely to be worthwhile to ask these questions in order to realize that they have not been answered. Even unanswered they may reveal the fact that no one could know, or at least that the informants could not know, the truth of the information given. Or they may suggest that a report *could* go back to satisfactory evidence but in its present state must depend on the untestable word of whoever produced it.

This particular consideration is likely to be of particular importance when considering reports which form part of the news of every day, but it is necessary to realize that even when serious and fully documented history is in question it is still necessary to remember the personality of the historian. As has been said when we look into the past we do not in fact see what happens to be there; unless we are actually engaged in historical research we see what a number of historians have said is there. They may have sincerely believed that theirs was a true and comprehensive account, but in fact what they reported will have unavoidably been coloured and moulded by factors personal to themselves—by the way they handled the evidence, by the measure of what they thought to be important, or to be probable or impossible, by their frame of reference and the significance they attached to certain phenomena, by their bias and probably by the historical myth, or anti-myth, in the terms of which they worked. All these things will have affected what they have had to say. If then opinions about history are going to be important it must be at least almost equally important to know something of those who have formed them. It is therefore not only desirable for people who are not historians to learn about the principles, habits and difficulties of historians in general, they should also know something of the particularities of those on whom they rely.

There is, however, a difficulty here. Most men and women are in fact influenced by a good many historical opinions of whose origin they know nothing. They have picked them up by the wayside. No doubt they started doing this at school when they studied history in a textbook, even the name of which they have probably forgotten. They will have gone on doing it ever since, assimilating, probably unconsciously, historical opinions from the dicta of politicians, from various forms of historical fiction, from casual conversation and from the natural prejudices of their class and race. It is difficult to know what to say about this. There can be no question of the danger of this habit. An engrained opinion which has never been reviewed or questioned is likely to strike a peculiarly deep root into the mind. If whoever holds it has lived with it for several years he is likely to have forgotten that it ever owed anything to human authorship; it will seem to be a self-evident truth and not an opinion which should be amenable to question and correction. As such it may acquire great power over the person who entertains it and be of great use to propagandists. Yet these habits are so natural and universal that little is gained by deploring them. All that can be done is to point out the dangers of anonymous history, and to urge that on important matters a revision of the historical assumptions which underlie even the most self-evident opinions may be of great value.

Such a revision must entail reading authoritative history books by known authors. But even these must be read critically. The best way to start doing this would be to get to know something about the authors and their historical traditions. But whether this is practicable or not, it should at the least be possible to watch carefully the way they use their evidence, particularly perhaps when they are making general statements about the characteristics and intentions of groups, since historians who are careful and scholarly when dealing with individual cases may well still use the old loose definitions and unsatisfactory methods when talking about groups. And even the best books should be read with the reservation that there is probably something relevant and important to be learnt from someone else.

If therefore reflection on the intrusions of history and the relevance of history emphasizes the great importance of the facts of history any historical experience should teach how difficult it is to be sure of them. There is no need to cavil at that. One of the objects of scholarship is to teach men and women when and how to be uncertain, how, that is, to be hesitant about much that is confidently asserted; or if it seems that something must be accepted to accept it tentatively and hypothetically as something which supplies a sufficient basis for action or thought, but is not sufficiently conclusive to close the mind. As I have said such an attitude should not be called sceptical. It is as well to remember how nearly allied to credulity are many forms of scepticism. The blind denial of a statement can be as irrational as the blind acceptance of one, the anti-myth may supply nearly as many over-simplifications and deceptive short-cuts to truth as the myth. Moreover scepticism may be curiously selective. Men will reject one section of a document basing their argument on facts drawn from another part of the same document. The fact that certain types of assertion have been bustled unceremoniously off the stage is often balanced by the fact that other equally unlikely assertions have been very easily accepted. Indeed it is significant that some examples of scepticism have led men to entertain some of the most unlikely beliefs that civilized men have ever entertained.

One reason for this strange phenomenon is worth a moment's attention. If any human transaction is examined with minute care and a full knowledge of what is going to result from it, it will often disclose a series of improbabilities, discrepancies and absurdities which do not seem to be explicable in the terms of the natural logic of events. They are probably minor abnormalities which in ordinary conditions it would be hardly worth noticing, coincidences which might seem rather strange if we forget that coincidences do happen, the results of the excentricity of character of one of the actors, the devastating consequences that normally result from human carelessness, incompetence or flurry. Or they are perfectly ordinary matters of which the explanation has been lost. But viewed under the microscope and with knowledge of what was going to happen they take on enormous proportions and a sinister meaning. It becomes impossible to believe that coincidences are coincidences. The ineptitudes caused by human incapacity and the silliness of bewildered action on the occurrence of a sudden emergency seem to require another and subtler explanation than simple human failure, and it becomes increasingly necessary to supply a meaning for everything that happened. As a result it becomes impossible to accept the ordinary simple account of the transaction in which such matters cannot be reconciled, and a more extravagant theory is accepted which, however improbable, seems to cover the facts.

There is what seems to be an example of this tendency in a book discussing the responsibility for the murder of President Lincoln.[1] The events leading up to and immediately following the murder are closely examined and seem to disclose an incompetence in guarding the President so great, and eccentricities in pursuit of the criminal so inexplicable, that some explanation which does not lie on the face of the facts seems called for; while some of those who were accused of having been accomplices were treated with such clumsy and vindictive injustice that it might look as if someone in authority wanted to divert attention from himself, or at the least had something to hide. As a result the author is inclined to believe in the existence of an undisclosed conspiracy to kill the President and the probability of the guilty complicity of one of Lincoln's own colleagues. What in fact the author appears to have left out of his calculations are the ordinary results of human carelessness and the cruel stupidities of passion after the event. There has been the same tendency to discover unacceptable discrepancies and improbabilities in the official account both of the events that led up to the murder of President Kennedy, and of those that followed it down to the murder of his murderer, and to suggest a conspiracy, probably with some official backing from some quarter.

[1] Otto Eisenschiml, *Why was Lincoln murdered?* (London, 1937).

In both of these cases the momentous results of the event seem to have led to an exaggeration of the unlikelihood, and therefore of the significance, of the admitted improbabilities in the story, though there is in fact no logical reason why an aberration should be more improbable because its consequences are important. There is an example of this tendency in 16th century England. I suppose it might in any circumstances have seemed to be worthy of remark that a relatively obscure actor from Stratford-on-Avon, not according to such records as have survived a well-educated man, should have succeeded in becoming a dramatist and a poet writing in the most polished style of his day. In ordinary circumstances, however, it seems likely that men would have concluded that the improbability is too slight, and that too many of the factors of the case are unknown, to make it necessary or desirable to try to find a complicated explanation. Since however the man was Shakespeare, who became possibly the greatest figure in all English literature, the facts have seemed to many people to be unacceptable and they have put forward the alternative supposition that the plays were really written by the great lawyer and philosopher Francis Bacon, who used 'the man from Stratford' as a stalking horse, and who indeed managed to conceal what was happening from Shakespeare's contemporaries, even those who knew Shakespeare personally, but revealed what he had done in a series of cryptograms hidden in the plays themselves.

There can, of course, be no rigid rules for the evaluation of evidence. Certainly there have been occasions when minor discrepancies in a narrative have led to doubts about its general truthfulness which subsequent research has justified, and sometimes what appeared at first to be a most extravagant explanation has been in due course verified. Nevertheless experience seems to shew that the scepticism which refuses to accept the simple explanation of something because it seems to contain improbabilities and inconsistencies is an uncertain guide. On the whole when there are points in the available account of a transaction which are not easily explicable it seems that it is more often better to accept provisionally the obvious explanation and to try to find more evidence to resolve its difficulties than to spend time and ingenuity in creating a complicated jigsaw puzzle into which all the facts, as they are known at the moment, can be forced. At the least it must be worthwhile to consider whether the improbability of too esoteric an explanation ought not to be a greater barrier to its acceptance than the contradictions and difficulties which made men reject a simpler conception. In any case what is only speculative ought not to be put forward as self evident or well-established fact. Readers of history should be on their guard against writers doing this, for it is a fairly common fault.

It is, then, important for everyone first to realize at what points history is likely to intrude into their lives, and secondly that they should become historians in order to be able to criticize the statements about history that present themselves to them. They must learn to ask the right questions of the evidence, to scrutinize with great care anyone from the most casual purveyor of gossip to the most solemn and laborious historian who claims to transmit historical information to them. And as historians they must recognize the great importance of another lesson. The significance of context. That is that words and events can only be understood in the terms of the situation in which they were spoken or enacted, that to take them from that context and present them in isolation is necessarily to falsify.

This is clearly true of words. A word may have had a meaning in a past period which it does not possess now. Or it may gain a special meaning from the transaction in which it is being used, or from the speaker or writer who uses and the occasion on which he uses it. Normally the sentence which contains it gains most of its meaning from what precedes it. In fact you cannot express an opinion on the significance of any particular word at any particular moment unless you know the context. The same is true of actions. Any action has its roots in the past. The forces of history will have prepared the circumstances in which the action took place and brought the actor into position. His own personal decision may have played some part in settling his role, or he may have had little choice, but it is certain that the situation in which he found himself will in large part have been provided by forces which were beyond his control. As the situation developed contingent events not of his motion will still further have limited the sphere of his decisions, and all the time to a greater or less extent his mind will have been shaped by the traditions of his period, of his race and of his class. No doubt he may have had some, perhaps considerable, freedom of choice, nevertheless circumstances which he had no hand in shaping will have dictated to him the limits within which his choices had to be made. To discuss his action without taking account of these limits must necessarily lead to misunderstanding and misjudgement.

This ought to be obvious, but it is often disregarded. An action is drawn from its context and then is judged by an absolute standard which takes no account of the circumstances of the moment and the way a man of that moment would regard those circumstances. A very common failure of those who judge the actions of the past is to forget the unavoidable ignorance of the actors, that they do no know much that is happening round them, and above all that they cannot know the future and the results of their actions. Too often also men and women of another century are rebuked for not having 20th century minds, or a situation is judged without regard to its complexity, and the fact that different circumstances have placed different parties to it in different positions, and that it is necessary to look at it from each of several positions to understand the ways in which the various actors throughout behaved.

Take for instance a situation which in the last thirty or forty years has been reasonably common, that of a nation emerging from dependent or colonial status and the scene of a conflict between a nationalist movement and the last controls of the occupying power. There will be various parties to such a situation. There will be the nationalist leaders. To them and probably to an increasing section of the population, the continued existence of any foreign control will seem to be an intolerable interference with their basic rights as human beings. To them any attempt to maintain the existing situation will seem to be mere oppression, and any step they may take to upset it will be legitimate warfare. In sharp contrast to these will be the soldiers and officials of the occupying power. It will be their task to do their duty as prescribed by their masters at home and part of their duty must be to keep order. For them the proper name for actions which their opponents call incidents in warfare may be 'terrorism', or 'murder'. In addition to this there may be sickening knowledge that minorities which have come to look to them for protection will be sure of maltreatment, possibly of massacre, as soon as the last foreign soldier leaves the country.

Another point of view may be present in the minds of the members of the government of the occupying power. They are likely to be pulled in two different directions. They have probably inherited the responsibility for the colony from an earlier generation, whose whole way of looking at such matters was different from what is acceptable today. Certainly as far as they can see it was men of their nation who converted a people which, through no fault of its own, was immersed in primitive conditions or at best got no further than a medieval polity, into a viable modern community; but that fact is in the past and not particularly relevant. Undoubtedly until recently men of their race governed the place with the apparent assent of all except a few irresponsible enthusiasts, but it is notorious that that situation has disappeared. There may be well-grounded fears about what may happen when they pull out, but the position will not get any better if they stay in, and they cannot go on for ever with a lively guerilla war on their hands and world opinion turning against them.

There will be other parties to such a situation. There will be the old-fashioned folk in the colony who saw nothing much to object to in the rule of the occupying power and are afraid of the changes the new nationalism may bring. There will be those who have served or supported the occupying power and may suffer in consequence. There will be the minorities to whom the occupying power seemed to have promised protection. Lastly there will be the simple people whose only object is to keep out of the way and avoid trouble.

Without trying to justify or condemn any of these groups it must be clear that it will be impossible even to understand the situation unless the threads behind each of them is carefully studied. But this is not only true of men involved in the tangled affairs of a territory on the eve of independence. It will be true of any man in any historical situation. Take any man in history of whom enough is known and calculate to what extent in a given situation his position and his actions were imposed on him by his circumstances and in what respects he was a free agent who could act as he wished, and then try to balance one against the other. I do not think that in most cases the result will add up to anything like an example of complete historical determinism, but I think the calculation will make it clear how wild will be your misjudgement of him unless you take his past and his circumstances into account.

All this is so obvious that it would be generally accepted but for one point. People do not normally go to history simply to understand; they are incurably moralistic. They want to praise or blame. They want to use history as a tribunal, and the plea of special circumstances might so diminish human responsibility that the tribunal could not sentence. This wish to appeal to the tribunal of history is a very natural one; very often the only vindication which helpless right can have against triumphant wrong is before the judgement seat of history. In many ways it is as well that man should hope for this vindication. The belief that here at least helpless right will be justified and powerful wrong condemned can be a healthy belief which has helped to sustain the conception of justice in human affairs. It has, however, too often helped to sustain other things as well. The desire to condemn does not always, probably does not normally, spring from an abstract desire for justice. Francis Bacon said that 'Revenge is a kind of wild justice'. Very often the desire for human justice is in essence a sombre and heavily moralized desire for revenge. The demand for justice at the bar of history is no exception to this. The motive behind it is very often the fact that those who feel it to be their duty to recount and stigmatize what they consider to have been the misdeeds of the past do so because in some way they identify themselves with the victims of those misdeeds and some other still existing group or historic personality with those who perpetrated them. Thereby hatred is sustained and increased.

Historical criticism can drain off some of this venom. It can destroy some of the legends which men have invented to barb their dislikes. It can keep before men's minds the difficulty of forming any reliable generalization about the intentions and ways of thought of large groups of people, particularly when most of them are dead and have left no record. It can emphasize the need to scrutinize carefully any evidence that may be offered in support of such generalizations. Above all it can encourage men to consider carefully the context of any important and controversial action, the extent to which the parts played by any of the actors, and the ways that they thought were determined for them by the processes of history, and so to realize how tragically often blind fate seems to throw men of reasonably goodwill against one another in incomprehending and apparently unavoidable conflict.

But the critical review of accepted history will by no means always eliminate, or modify, the statements of fact and the opinions about history which create hatred. If it is honest, and it is of no use to anyone if it is not, it will confirm the fact that there are transactions in the human record quite as horrible as they were reported to be and that men and women have been inspired by motives, or cultivated habits of mind, which must be called evil, if the word evil is ever to be used by one human being of another. If anyone doubts this he had better consider the case of those who were guilty for the murder, largely in cold blood, often after humiliation and torture, of about six million Jews, men, women *and* children, between 1939–45. History cannot be silent about this, and, unless the tribunal of history is a phantasy and a myth, it must pass judgement; though a study of the trials of some of the war criminals, particularly of some of the minor ones, may suggest how difficult are some of the moral problems which judgement involves. Fortunately these problems can perhaps be left with propriety to people who are not primarily historians, to jurists, to philosophers, to theologians or perhaps to psychologists; the historian's task is completed when he has described what he thinks happened and, as far as history can reveal this, why it happened.

This is in all conscience hard enough. The historian must not gloze over ugly things, or avoid calling them by their proper names. He must try not to take sides, and there is a great temptation to take sides in matters which cause high emotional tension, and on which other people are vehemently taking sides. He must of course try to get as near to the truth of the relevant events as is possible, and try to analyse their historical background. All this he must do without fear or favour, or an attempt to spare anyone's feelings. To do otherwise would be to fail in his duty and, among other things, fail to reveal the dangerous propensities of the human race.

This leads back to a principle which must underlie all that I have written. The criticism of history can, so I believe, be of value in a number of ways, but its primary object must be to get nearer the truth that lies behind any historical opinion that is worth considering. If that is not the primary object of the critic, if he is trying to do something else without regard for that object, even if what he is trying to do is to disperse the historical opinions which create hatred, his work will be worth nothing. It is in the last resort its relation to truth that gives history its value. History can serve a number of purposes. It can amuse, it can instruct, it can warn, it can encourage, it can provide the data for important decisions and it can help in the analysis of society. But it can do none of these things if it is not conscientiously aimed at the truth, for in that case it is not history but a fraud.

This is true if history is asked, as it is so often asked, to pass judgement on past misdeeds. I ought to say that I do not myself believe that judgements on dead people can ever be satisfactory. It is not in my belief possible to know enough of the circumstances of those on whom they are to be pronounced, nor is it possible to detach oneself from the issues of any historical conflict sufficiently effectively to be capable of doing equal justice to all the people concerned. I hold that it is desirable to stigmatize evil deeds but not to condemn people, and that in general the historian serves the general interests of mankind better if he tries to understand and to explain than if he assumes the position of a judge.[1] Whether there is to be another judgement elsewhere, where there is greater knowledge and greater detachment, is a problem which does not come within the terms of this argument. However my opinion is not shared by a great number of people who eagerly look to history for justice and it is important not to satisfy one's own conscience

---

[1] See G. Kitson Clark, *The Kingdom of Free Men* (Cambridge University Press, 1957), Cap VI, where I have tried to discuss the grounds for this opinion.

by generously passing over the misdeeds from which others have suffered. I would not therefore wish my personal opinion to divert attention from what is the main point here; for both the historian who wishes to understand and the historian who wishes to judge there is the same primary necessity. They must both try to get as near to the truth of any matter that they are considering as they can.

Historical criticism is offered as an instrument formed to enable human beings to get nearer the truth. It does this by attempting to test the relationship between what purports to be history and the truth which lies behind it. It probes the evidence which it is claimed is the link between an historical opinion and reality. It promotes an analysis of the conceptions in which an historical opinion is expressed and draws attention to the significance of the personality of the historian. The result may be to confirm what is already believed, or to produce something which is altogether more coherent and convincing, or it may be to destroy altogether anything that seemed to be certain or made sense. Even so it will have value for it may be that the only knowledge which can at the moment be trusted on a particular subject is that nothing is known about it, and possibly that, as far as can be foreseen, nothing more coherent or certain will ever be known about it. To realize so much is also a step towards reality, and the need to bring as near as is possible to the test of reality those assertions about history which present themselves so continually to us and play such an important part in our lives is the justification for the consideration of those matters which I have tried to discuss in this book.

Index